Learn Mexican Spanish In Your Car

100 Days To Fluency Through Engaging Lessons, Essential Verbs, And Everyday Slang For Beginners

Javier Caminos

COPYRIGHT

Copyright © 2024 by Javier Caminos

All rights reserved. No part of this publication may be reproduced, distributed, or transmitted in any form or by any means, including photocopying, recording, or other electronic or mechanical methods, without the prior written permission of the publisher, except in the case of brief quotations embodied in critical reviews and certain other noncommercial uses permitted by copyright law.

First Edition

Identifiers: ISBN 9798321661161 (paperback) | ISBN 9798321663783 (hardcover)

Names: Caminos, Javier, author.

Title: Learn Mexican Spanish In Your Car: 100 Days To Fluency Through Engaging Lessons, Essential Verbs, And Everyday Slang For Beginners / Javier Caminos

DISCLAIMER

The books authored by Javier Caminos are provided for educational and informational purposes only. These materials are intended to assist learners in their journey towards Spanish fluency and are designed to be used as supplementary learning tools alongside formal education, practice, and immersion experiences.

While Javier Caminos has made every effort to ensure the accuracy and effectiveness of the content provided in his books, the learning outcomes may vary significantly among individuals due to differences in learning styles, dedication, prior knowledge, and access to additional educational resources. As such, the author cannot guarantee fluency within a specific timeframe or as a result of following the book's guidance alone.

Readers are encouraged to approach the learning process with patience and persistence, recognizing that language acquisition is a complex and gradual process that differs for each individual. These books do not purport to be a comprehensive solution to language learning, nor do they replace the need for professional instruction, certification, or real-world language usage.

Javier Caminos and the publisher disclaim all liability for any loss, damage, injury, or expense however caused, arising from the use of or reliance upon, in any manner, the information provided through his books, suggesting that readers should always consult with a qualified educator or language professional for advice tailored to their specific learning needs and objectives.

By utilizing these books, readers accept and agree that any language learning endeavor involves inherent challenges and agree not to hold the author or publisher responsible for any misunderstandings, miscommunications, or misinterpretations that may occur from the use of the materials provided.

This disclaimer is to be regarded as part of the terms and conditions for the use of Javier Caminos' language learning books.

TABLE OF CONTENTS

Preface..9
Part 1: Days 1-10 - Basics of Mexican Spanish...............................18
Day 1: Introduction to Mexican Spanish Pronunciation...................19
Day 2: Basic Greetings and Essentials...22
Day 3: Numbers and Time...25
Day 4: Common Verbs and Their Conjugations.............................29
Day 5: Creating Simple Sentences..33
Days 6-10: Review of Basics and Practical Application..................36
Part 2: Days 11-20 - Building Conversational Foundations.............39
Day 11: Nouns, Articles, and Adjectives...40
Day 12: Forming Questions and Answers.......................................43
Day 13: Everyday Activities and Routines......................................46
Day 14: Describing People and Places..49
Day 15: Ordering Food and Dining Out..52
Days 16-20: Conversational Foundations Review...........................55
Part 3: Days 21-30 - Navigating Daily Situations...........................58
Day 21: Directions, Transportation, and Getting Around................59
Day 22: Shopping and Transactions..62
Day 23: Making Plans and Appointments.......................................65
Day 24: Expressing Likes, Dislikes, and Preferences......................68
Day 25: Cultural Norms and Social Etiquette.................................71

Days 26-30: Daily Situations Review and Practice..........................74

Part 4: Days 31-40 - Exploring Grammar and Structure.................77

Day 31: Introduction to Tenses: Present, Past, and Future..............78

Day 32: Modal Verbs and Useful Expressions................................82

Day 33: The Imperative Mood and Giving Commands...................85

Day 34: Adverbs and Frequency..88

Day 35: Prepositions and Location...91

Days 36-40: Grammar Deep Dive Review......................................94

Part 5: Days 41-50 - Deepening Vocabulary and Usage.................97

Day 41: Family and Relationships..98

Day 42: Work and Professional Life...101

Day 43: Education and Schooling...104

Day 44: Health, Wellness, and Emergencies................................107

Day 45: Leisure, Entertainment, and Sports.................................111

Days 46-50: Vocabulary Expansion Review.................................115

Part 6: Days 51-60 - Mexican Culture and Slang.........................118

Day 51: Festivals and Holidays..119

Day 52: Food and Culinary Traditions..122

Day 53: Music, Dance, and Art...125

Day 54: Regional Differences and Dialects..................................128

Day 55: Slang and Everyday Expressions....................................131

Days 56-60: Cultural Immersion Review......................................134

Part 7: Days 61-70 - Advanced Conversational Skills..................137

Day 61: Advanced Dialogue Construction...................................138

Day 62: Subjunctive Mood and Expressing Doubt or Desire.........141

Day 63: Narrating Stories and Past Events.................................144
Day 64: Discussing Future Plans and Hypotheticals....................147
Day 65: Persuading and Negotiating..150
Days 66-70: Advanced Communication Review.........................153
Part 8: Days 71-80 - Practical Applications for Fluency...............156
Day 71: Problem Solving in Spanish..157
Day 72: Making Complaints and Resolving Conflicts..................160
Day 73: Planning Events and Hosting..163
Day 74: Traveling and Adventure...166
Day 75: Technology and the Internet...170
Days 76-80: Real-World Spanish Use Review...............................173
Part 9: Days 81-90 - Professional and Technical Spanish..............176
Day 81: Business and Commerce Language...................................177
Day 82: Technical Terms for IT and Digital Media.......................181
Day 83: Medical Spanish for Healthcare..185
Day 84: Spanish for Educators and Students.................................189
Day 85: Legal Spanish and Understanding Contracts....................193
Days 86-90: Professional Language Skills Review........................197
Part 10: Days 91-100 - Mastery and Beyond.................................200
Day 91: Creative Writing and Storytelling.....................................201
Day 92: Debates, Opinions, and Critical Thinking........................204
Day 93: Public Speaking and Presentations...................................207
Day 94: Understanding and Analyzing Media...............................211
Day 95: The Path to Bilingualism – Next Steps............................215
Days 96-100: Final Review and Path Forward..............................218

Appendix A: Commonly Confused Words..................................221

Appendix B: Verb Conjugation Tables.......................................225

Appendix C: Mexican Spanish vs. Spain Spanish.......................228

Glossary of Terms..231

About The Author..237

PREFACE

Introduction to the Book

Welcome to "Learn Mexican Spanish In Your Car: 100 Days To Fluency Through Engaging Lessons, Essential Verbs, And Everyday Slang For Beginners." This book is designed with one primary goal in mind: to help you achieve fluency in Mexican Spanish in a convenient, efficient, and engaging way. Whether you're a busy professional, a student, or someone who spends a considerable amount of time commuting, this book is tailored to fit seamlessly into your lifestyle, enabling you to make the most of your time on the move.

Mexican Spanish is a vibrant and rich language, full of expressions, nuances, and cultural depth that makes it uniquely appealing. This book focuses on the Mexican variant of Spanish, providing you with the linguistic tools and cultural insights necessary to communicate effectively and authentically within a Mexican context. From the bustling streets of Mexico City to the scenic landscapes of Oaxaca, the language skills you acquire through this book will serve as your bridge to the heart and soul of Mexico.

Why learn Spanish in your car? For many of us, our cars are not just vehicles but spaces where we spend a significant portion of our day—often wishing we could use that time more productively. "Learn Mexican Spanish In Your Car" transforms your commute into an immersive learning experience. Through a carefully structured program of lessons, reviews, and practical exercises, you will progress from basic greetings and phrases to advanced conversational fluency, all without needing to alter your daily routine.

This book is structured into ten parts, each spanning ten days, with a focus on lessons during the first five days and comprehensive reviews in the latter half. Each lesson is designed to be engaging and accessible, with clear explanations, practical examples, and tips for pronunciation. The review sessions consolidate what you've learned, reinforcing your knowledge and boosting your confidence.

By the end of these 100 days, you will not only have a solid foundation in Mexican Spanish but also an appreciation for Mexico's rich culture, traditions, and way of life. You'll learn not just how to construct sentences but how to express yourself in ways that resonate with the Mexican spirit—whether it's ordering your favorite dish at a local taqueria, navigating the colorful markets, or engaging in meaningful conversations with friends.

So, buckle up and prepare for a journey that promises not just to teach you a language but to open up a world of new experiences, connections, and opportunities. Welcome to your first step towards fluency in Mexican Spanish. Let's make every moment count.

How To Use This Book

"Learn Mexican Spanish In Your Car: 100 Days To Fluency Through Engaging Lessons, Essential Verbs, And Everyday Slang For Beginners" is more than just a guide; it's your companion on the road to mastering Mexican Spanish. This section will help you navigate through the book effectively, ensuring that every minute you spend with it brings you closer to your goal of fluency. Here's how to make the most of this book:

Set Your Learning Environment

Ideally, your car should be a place of focus and learning. Before you start each lesson, ensure that you're in a safe and comfortable setting where you can listen, repeat, and reflect without distractions or interruptions. If you're not in your car, find a quiet space where you can emulate a focused learning environment.

Daily Lessons and Practice

The book is structured into daily lessons, each designed to be completed in about 20-30 minutes—the perfect length for most commutes. Days 1-5 of each 10-day segment introduce new topics or vocabulary. Engage with each lesson actively by repeating phrases out loud, practicing the pronunciation, and mentally constructing your own sentences using the day's learning material.

Review and Reinforcement

Days 6-10 focus on reviewing the content from the previous five days, consolidating your learning through repetition, and applying the knowledge in practical contexts. These review days are crucial for reinforcing your memory and understanding of the language.

Use the Supplementary Materials

The appendices and index at the end of the book are there to support your learning. They include verb conjugation tables, a glossary of terms, and a section on commonly confused words. Refer to these materials regularly to clarify doubts or reinforce your learning.

Engage with the Exercises

The practical exercises are designed to simulate real-life conversations and situations you might encounter in Mexico. These are your opportunities to apply what you've learned in a practical context, enhancing both your comprehension and your speaking skills.

Track Your Progress

At the end of each 10-day part, take a moment to reflect on what you've learned and how comfortable you feel with the material. Use the assessment and reflection sections to gauge your progress and identify areas where you might need additional practice.

Be Consistent

Consistency is key to language learning. Try to engage with the book at the same time each day, turning your lesson into a habit. Even on days when you can't be in your car or dedicate a full session to study, review your notes or think in Spanish to keep the language at the forefront of your mind.

Embrace Mistakes

Learning a new language is a journey filled with challenges and mistakes. Embrace these as part of the learning process. Each error is an opportunity to improve and deepen your understanding of Mexican Spanish.

Supplement Your Learning

While this book is comprehensive, supplementing your studies with additional materials such as Spanish music, podcasts, and conversations with native speakers can enhance your learning experience and expose you to the language's richness and variety.

By following these guidelines, you will maximize your learning experience with this book. Remember, the journey to fluency is a marathon, not a sprint. Patience, perseverance, and practice are your best tools on this journey. Welcome aboard, and enjoy the ride to fluency in Mexican Spanish!

The Benefits of Learning Spanish in Your Car

Embarking on the journey to learn a new language can be daunting, especially when trying to fit it into a busy schedule. "Learn Mexican Spanish In Your Car: 100 Days To Fluency Through Engaging Lessons, Essential Verbs, And Everyday Slang For Beginners" leverages the time spent in your car—a space many of us use daily but rarely consider a place of learning. Here are the key benefits of adopting this approach to language learning:

Efficient Use of Time

For many, the daily commute is a significant part of the day that often feels unproductive. Learning Spanish in your car transforms this idle time into an invaluable opportunity for personal growth and education. It's a way to make your commute work for you, turning what may have been a frustration into a productive and enriching part of your day.

Safe, Distraction-Free Environment

Your car is a personal space where you can focus without the distractions common to home or public spaces. It provides a controlled environment where you can repeat phrases aloud, listen to pronunciation, and practice your speaking skills without self-consciousness or interruption.

Enhanced Retention Through Repetition

Audio-based learning, especially in a setting where you can listen and then immediately repeat and practice, greatly enhances language retention. The repetition of phrases and sentences in a focused setting like your car helps solidify your understanding and recall of the language.

Integration into Daily Routine

Incorporating language learning into your daily routine increases the likelihood of consistency and long-term commitment. Since driving is already a part of your daily habit, adding Spanish lessons into this routine creates a natural and sustainable learning path.

Contextual Learning

Learning in your car, a place where you might actually use Spanish to navigate or interact with others, places your lessons in a practical context. It prepares you for real-world situations, such as asking for directions, ordering food, or having a casual conversation, making the learning experience more relevant and immediate.

Personalized Pace

In your car, you control the pace of your learning. You can replay lessons as needed, spend extra time on challenging concepts, or skip ahead if you're comfortable with the material. This self-paced approach respects your individual learning speed and needs, making it a highly personalized experience.

Reduced Pressure and Anxiety

Learning in the privacy of your car reduces the anxiety and pressure that can come with language learning, especially speaking. The solitude allows you to practice without fear of judgment, encouraging more practice and experimentation with pronunciation and sentence structure.

Preparation for Real-life Use

Finally, learning Spanish in your car prepares you for the real-life application of the language. Whether you're planning a trip to Mexico, looking to connect with Spanish-speaking friends or colleagues, or simply aiming to broaden your cultural horizons, this book equips you with practical language skills that are immediately applicable outside the confines of your vehicle.

By learning Spanish in your car, you're not just acquiring a new language; you're also making smart use of your time, creating a habit that fits seamlessly into your life, and setting the stage for a rewarding journey towards fluency in Mexican Spanish.

Overview of Mexican Spanish

Mexican Spanish, while sharing the core of its vocabulary and grammar with the Spanish spoken in Spain and other Spanish-speaking countries, has its own unique characteristics, expressions, and nuances that reflect the rich cultural heritage and history of Mexico. This section provides an overview of Mexican Spanish, highlighting what makes it distinct and why it's a fascinating variant of the language to learn.

Linguistic Richness and Diversity

Mexico's linguistic landscape is profoundly influenced by its indigenous languages and cultures, as well as its historical interactions with European and other languages. This rich tapestry is reflected in the vocabulary, idiomatic expressions, and even the pronunciation of Mexican Spanish. Words borrowed from Nahuatl (the language of the Aztecs) and other indigenous languages are commonly used, enriching the language with terms that have no direct equivalents in other Spanish-speaking countries.

Pronunciation and Accent

Mexican Spanish is known for its clear pronunciation and relatively neutral accent, especially compared to other Spanish dialects. This clarity makes it an excellent variant for learners of Spanish. The intonation and rhythm of Mexican Spanish are distinctive, with a melodious quality that many learners find appealing and accessible.

Vocabulary and Expressions

One of the most delightful aspects of learning Mexican Spanish is the discovery of its unique vocabulary and expressions. Mexican Spanish includes a wealth of colloquialisms, slang, and idioms that vividly express emotions, describe situations, and create a sense of camaraderie among speakers. These expressions often carry cultural references that offer insights into the Mexican way of life, humor, and values.

Cultural Context

Language and culture are inseparably intertwined. Learning Mexican Spanish opens a window to understanding Mexico's cultural traditions, social norms, and historical context. From the deeply rooted family values and the significance of religious and national holidays to the contemporary issues and the vibrant arts and culinary scene, Mexican Spanish is a gateway to engaging with Mexico's rich cultural heritage.

Regional Variations

Within Mexico, there are regional variations in accent, vocabulary, and even grammar. These differences reflect the country's geographical diversity and cultural richness. While this book focuses on a standard Mexican Spanish that is understood across the country, learners will also be introduced to some of these regional characteristics, enhancing their appreciation of the language's diversity.

Practicality and Global Relevance

Mexican Spanish is not only the variant spoken by the majority of Spanish speakers in North America but also one of the most influential globally due to Mexico's economic, cultural, and demographic significance. Learning Mexican Spanish not only prepares you to communicate effectively with Spanish speakers in Mexico and the United States but also enriches your global perspective and intercultural competence.

In summary, Mexican Spanish is a vibrant, accessible, and richly expressive variant of the Spanish language. Through this book, you will embark on a journey that not only teaches you how to communicate in Mexican Spanish but also immerses you in the cultural nuances that make Mexico a country of profound beauty, complexity, and warmth. Welcome to the vibrant world of Mexican Spanish.

Part 1: Days 1-10 - Basics of Mexican Spanish

Day 1: Introduction to Mexican Spanish Pronunciation

Welcome to Day 1 of your journey to fluency in Mexican Spanish. Today, we focus on the foundational aspect of any language learning adventure: pronunciation. Understanding and practicing the sounds of Mexican Spanish from the outset will set the stage for effective communication and enhance your ability to understand and be understood. Here's what you need to know to get started.

The Spanish Alphabet

Mexican Spanish uses the same 27 letters as the rest of the Spanish-speaking world, plus the "ñ." Each letter has a distinct name and sound, some of which might be unfamiliar if you're coming from an English-speaking background. Pay special attention to vowels, as their clear, consistent pronunciation is crucial to Mexican Spanish.

Vowels

The vowels in Mexican Spanish — a, e, i, o, u — are pronounced more sharply and consistently than in English. Here's a quick guide:

- **A** sounds like 'ah' as in "father."
- **E** sounds like 'eh' as in "bed."
- **I** sounds like 'ee' as in "see."
- **O** sounds like 'oh' as in "low."

- **U** sounds like 'oo' as in "food."

Consonants

Most consonants are pronounced similarly to English, but with less aspiration. Key differences include:

- **B/V** are pronounced nearly identically, somewhere between the English 'b' and 'v.'
- **J** and **G** (before e or i) produce a strong, raspy sound similar to the 'h' in "ha."
- **LL** and **Y** often sound like the 'y' in "yes," although in some regions, they can sound like the 'j' in "jeep."
- **Ñ** represents a unique sound not found in English, similar to the 'ny' in "canyon."
- **R** is trilled or rolled, a sound that can take some practice for new learners. A single **R** at the beginning of a word or double **RR** is strongly trilled, while a single **R** between vowels is lightly tapped.

Syllable Stress

In Mexican Spanish, the stress or emphasis placed on syllables can change the meaning of words. While specific rules determine stress placement, a general rule is that if a word ends in a vowel, "n," or "s," the stress falls on the penultimate (second to last) syllable. If it ends in a consonant (other than "n" or "s"), the stress is on the last syllable. Accented vowels break these rules and always receive stress.

Practice Makes Perfect

Listening and repeating are your best tools for mastering pronunciation. Practice with these common phrases, paying close attention to vowel sounds and syllable stress:

- **Hola** (Hello) - oh-lah

- **Buenos días** (Good morning) - bwe-nos dee-as

- **¿Cómo estás?** (How are you?) - koh-moh eh-stahs?

- **Mucho gusto** (Nice to meet you) - moo-choh goos-toh

- **Adiós** (Goodbye) - ah-dee-ohs

Listening Exercise

Engage with authentic Mexican Spanish as much as possible. Listen to music, watch movies, or find podcasts that suit your interests. Pay attention to how speakers pronounce the vowels and consonants, and try to mimic the rhythm and melody of their speech.

Congratulations on completing Day 1! Remember, pronunciation is a skill that improves with practice, so don't hesitate to repeat these exercises and listen to as much Mexican Spanish as you can. See you on Day 2, where we'll dive into basic greetings and essentials. ¡Hasta mañana!

Day 2: Basic Greetings and Essentials

On Day 2 of our journey, we dive into the heart of any conversation: greetings and essential phrases. Mastering these will not only boost your confidence but also enable you to start and navigate basic interactions in Mexican Spanish. Let's explore the fundamental greetings and essential expressions that are key to everyday conversations.

Greetings Throughout the Day

In Mexico, as in many cultures, greetings vary depending on the time of day:

- **Buenos días** (Good morning) - Used from sunrise until noon.

- **Buenas tardes** (Good afternoon) - Used from noon until the evening (around 7 PM or sunset).

- **Buenas noches** (Good evening/Good night) - Used from the evening until sunrise, both for greeting and saying goodbye.

Meeting Someone New

When you meet someone for the first time, it's polite to use the following expressions:

- **Mucho gusto** (Nice to meet you) - A universal phrase used upon the first introduction.

- **¿Cómo te llamas?** (What's your name?) - For informal situations. In formal contexts, use **¿Cómo se llama?**

- **Me llamo...** (My name is...) - Use this phrase to introduce yourself.

Asking How Someone Is

Showing interest in how someone is feeling is a common way to continue a conversation:

- **¿Cómo estás?** (How are you?) - For informal situations. Use **¿Cómo está?** for formal contexts.

- **Bien, gracias. ¿Y tú?** (Well, thank you. And you?) - A common response when you're doing well. In formal situations, replace **¿Y tú?** with **¿Y usted?**

Politeness Phrases

These are essential in any language to show respect and good manners:

- **Por favor** (Please) - Adds politeness to any request.

- **Gracias** (Thank you) - Never forget to express gratitude.

- **De nada** (You're welcome) - The standard response to **Gracias**.

- **Lo siento** (I'm sorry) - Use this to apologize or express regret.

- **Disculpa** (Excuse me) - For getting someone's attention or apologizing in informal contexts. Use **Disculpe** for formal situations.

Saying Goodbye

Concluding conversations gracefully is just as important as starting them:

- **Adiós** (Goodbye) - A universal way to say goodbye.
- **Hasta luego** (See you later) - Implies you'll see the person again.
- **Nos vemos** (See you) - A casual way to say goodbye.

Practice Conversation

Try practicing these simple exchanges with a friend or language partner:

- **A:** ¡Hola! ¿Cómo estás?
- **B:** Hola, bien, gracias. ¿Y tú?
- **A:** Muy bien, gracias. Me llamo [Your Name]. ¿Y tú, cómo te llamas?
- **B:** Me llamo [Partner's Name]. Mucho gusto.
- **A:** El gusto es mío.

Cultural Tip

In Mexico, greetings often involve a handshake, a hug, or a cheek kiss (mostly among women and between men and women), depending on the level of intimacy. While using these phrases, adopting the accompanying social customs can help convey warmth and friendliness.

Congratulations on completing Day 2! With these greetings and essential phrases, you're now equipped to begin and end conversations in Mexican Spanish. Keep practicing, and remember, repetition is the key to mastery. Tomorrow, we'll explore numbers, days of the week, and telling time. ¡Hasta mañana!

Day 3: Numbers and Time

Welcome to Day 3! Today's lesson is all about numbers, days of the week, and how to tell time in Mexican Spanish. These are fundamental components of everyday conversation, from asking for prices and giving your phone number to making plans. Let's dive in!

Numbers 1-20

Let's start with the basics. Here are the numbers from 1 to 20, which form the foundation for most numerical expressions:

1. Uno
2. Dos
3. Tres
4. Cuatro
5. Cinco
6. Seis
7. Siete
8. Ocho
9. Nueve
10. Diez
11. Once
12. Doce
13. Trece

14. Catorce

15. Quince

16. Dieciséis

17. Diecisiete

18. Dieciocho

19. Diecinueve

20. Veinte

Practice saying these numbers out loud until you feel comfortable with them.

Days of the Week

Knowing the days of the week is crucial for planning and scheduling. In Spanish, the week starts with Monday:

- Lunes (Monday)
- Martes (Tuesday)
- Miércoles (Wednesday)
- Jueves (Thursday)
- Viernes (Friday)
- Sábado (Saturday)
- Domingo (Sunday)

Telling Time

Telling time in Spanish is straightforward. The basic structure is "Son las [hour] y [minutes]." For 1 o'clock, use "Es la una."

- **¿Qué hora es?** (What time is it?)
- **Son las dos** (It's 2:00).
- **Es la una y cuarto** (It's 1:15).
- **Son las cuatro y media** (It's 4:30).

For minutes past 30, you can subtract from the next hour, using "menos" (minus). For example, 3:45 can be said as **"Son las cuatro menos cuarto."**

Practice Phrases

Here are some practice phrases incorporating numbers and time:

- **Tengo dos hermanos** (I have two siblings).
- **Mi número de teléfono es...** (My phone number is...).
- **Nos vemos el sábado** (See you on Saturday).
- **La reunión es a las tres y media** (The meeting is at 3:30).

Cultural Insight

Time in Mexican culture can be flexible. When making social plans, it's not uncommon for things to start a bit later than scheduled. However, for formal appointments or business settings, punctuality is appreciated.

Exercise

Try creating sentences with different numbers, days, and times. For example, plan a hypothetical week in Spanish, including activities, meetings, and leisure time.

Congratulations on completing Day 3! You're now able to discuss numbers, days, and time in Mexican Spanish, opening up a wide range of conversational topics. Keep practicing, and soon these will become second nature. Tomorrow, we'll explore common verbs and their conjugations to start building more complex sentences. ¡Hasta entonces!

Day 4: Common Verbs and Their Conjugations

Welcome to Day 4, where we'll focus on common verbs and their conjugations in Mexican Spanish. Verbs are the backbone of communication, allowing us to express actions, states of being, and desires. Today, we'll introduce some essential verbs and how to conjugate them in the present tense, providing you with the tools to start forming your own sentences.

The Importance of Verbs

In Spanish, verbs are conjugated to align with the subject of the sentence. This means the verb changes form depending on who is performing the action. Today, we'll concentrate on the present tense, which is used to describe current actions or states.

Essential Verbs

Let's look at some essential verbs that you'll find yourself using in everyday conversations:

- **Ser** (to be) - Describes essential qualities or characteristics.

- **Estar** (to be) - Used for states or conditions, often temporary.

- **Tener** (to have) - Expresses possession or age.

- **Ir** (to go) - Indicates movement or future plans with "a."

Conjugation Patterns

Spanish verbs fall into three categories based on their infinitive endings: -ar, -er, and -ir. Each group has its own conjugation pattern. Here, we'll introduce the present tense conjugation for each of the essential verbs mentioned:

- **Ser (to be)**
    - Yo soy (I am)
    - Tú eres (You are, familiar)
    - Él/Ella/Usted es (He/She/You are, formal)
    - Nosotros somos (We are)
    - Ellos/Ellas/Ustedes son (They/You all are)

- **Estar (to be)**
    - Yo estoy (I am)
    - Tú estás (You are, familiar)
    - Él/Ella/Usted está (He/She/You are, formal)
    - Nosotros estamos (We are)
    - Ellos/Ellas/Ustedes están (They/You all are)

- **Tener (to have)**
    - Yo tengo (I have)
    - Tú tienes (You have, familiar)
    - Él/Ella/Usted tiene (He/She/You have, formal)
    - Nosotros tenemos (We have)
    - Ellos/Ellas/Ustedes tienen (They/You all have)

- **Ir (to go)**
  - Yo voy (I go)
  - Tú vas (You go, familiar)
  - Él/Ella/Usted va (He/She/You go, formal)
  - Nosotros vamos (We go)
  - Ellos/Ellas/Ustedes van (They/You all go)

Forming Sentences

With these verbs, you can start forming basic sentences. Here are some examples:

- **Yo soy estudiante.** (I am a student.)
- **Ella está feliz hoy.** (She is happy today.)
- **Nosotros tenemos dos perros.** (We have two dogs.)
- **Vamos al cine mañana.** (We are going to the cinema tomorrow.)

Practice Exercise

Try conjugating these verbs with different subjects and creating your own sentences. For example, use **tener** to talk about things you have or **ir** to describe where you're going.

Cultural Note

Verbs and expressions of being, such as **ser** and **estar**, are central to expressing identity and emotions in Mexican culture. Paying attention to their use can offer deeper insights into the Mexican way of life and values.

Congratulations on completing Day 4! You're now equipped with some of the most essential verbs in Spanish and understand how to conjugate them in the present tense. Practice these conjugations, and try forming sentences on your own. Tomorrow, we'll expand on this foundation by exploring how to create simple sentences, bringing us one step closer to conversational fluency. ¡Nos vemos mañana!

Day 5: Creating Simple Sentences

Congratulations on reaching Day 5! By now, you've dipped your toes into the waters of Mexican Spanish pronunciation, learned essential greetings, counted to twenty, and familiarized yourself with some of the most common verbs. Today, we're going to use those building blocks to start forming simple sentences. Constructing sentences is where the magic of language comes alive—allowing you to communicate ideas, share thoughts, and connect with others.

Subject-Verb-Object (SVO) Structure

The basic structure of most sentences in Spanish follows the Subject-Verb-Object (SVO) order, similar to English. Understanding this structure will help you form coherent and grammatically correct sentences. For example:

- **Yo tengo un libro.** (I have a book.)

- **Ella es profesora.** (She is a teacher.)

Using Adjectives

Adjectives describe nouns and in Spanish, they usually come after the noun they describe. Unlike English, adjectives in Spanish must agree in gender and number with the nouns they describe. For example:

- **Un perro pequeño** (A small dog) - masculine singular

- **Una casa grande** (A big house) - feminine singular

Forming Questions

To form questions in Spanish, you often only need to change the intonation of your statement and add question marks. You can also start questions with question words like **¿Qué?** (What?), **¿Dónde?** (Where?), and **¿Cómo?** (How?). For example:

- **¿Tú tienes un libro?** (Do you have a book?)
- **¿Dónde está el baño?** (Where is the bathroom?)

Using Negation

To make a sentence negative in Spanish, place **no** before the verb. For example:

- **Yo no tengo un libro.** (I do not have a book.)
- **Ella no es profesora.** (She is not a teacher.)

Practice Forming Sentences

Now, let's practice what you've learned by forming some simple sentences. Use the verbs and vocabulary from the previous days to create sentences following the SVO structure. Remember to make your adjectives agree with the nouns they describe.

Example Sentences

- **Yo soy estudiante.** (I am a student.)
- **Nosotros vamos al cine.** (We are going to the cinema.)
- **Ellos tienen una casa grande.** (They have a big house.)

Cultural Insight

When creating sentences, it's important to remember that formality in language reflects respect in many Hispanic cultures, including Mexico. Using the formal **usted** instead of **tú** in certain situations can show respect for elders or people you're not familiar with.

Exercise

Try to create sentences describing yourself, your family, or your surroundings using the SVO structure. Experiment with making questions and negative sentences as well.

Congratulations on completing Day 5! You're now able to put together simple sentences in Mexican Spanish, a crucial step towards fluency. Keep practicing, and don't be afraid to experiment with the vocabulary and structures you've learned so far. Tomorrow, we'll begin our first review session, where we'll reinforce and expand upon what you've learned this week. ¡Hasta mañana!

DAYS 6-10: REVIEW OF BASICS AND PRACTICAL APPLICATION

Welcome to the first review and practice session of your journey to fluency in Mexican Spanish! Over the past five days, you've laid the foundation by learning pronunciation, essential greetings, numbers, time, common verbs, and the basics of sentence structure. Now, it's time to reinforce what you've learned, correct any misunderstandings, and start applying your knowledge in practical contexts. This five-day review is designed to consolidate your skills and build your confidence in using Mexican Spanish for real-life communication.

Day 6: Pronunciation and Greetings Refresher

- **Revisit Pronunciation:** Practice the sounds that are unique to Mexican Spanish, especially the vowels and the rolled "r." Use tongue twisters and repeat phrases you found challenging.

- **Greetings Practice:** Go through all the greetings you've learned, saying them out loud. Practice both formal and informal situations, and remember to use the correct greeting depending on the time of day.

Day 7: Numbers, Days, and Telling Time

- **Numbers Drill:** Challenge yourself to count to 100, focusing on any numbers that are difficult to remember. Try incorporating numbers into sentences, like talking about your age, how many siblings you have, or how many items you want to buy.

- **Days and Time Practice:** Schedule your week in Spanish, including activities for each day. Practice asking and telling time, making appointments, or planning meetings in Spanish.

Day 8: Verb Conjugation and Sentence Formation

- **Verb Review:** Revisit the verbs "ser," "estar," "tener," and "ir." Conjugate each verb in the present tense for all subjects, and create sentences with each conjugation.

- **Sentence Structure Exercise:** Combine what you've learned about nouns, verbs, and adjectives to create more complex sentences. Describe yourself, your friends, or family members using the verbs you've practiced.

Day 9: Practical Application Through Dialogues

- **Create Dialogues:** Use the phrases and sentence structures you've learned to write dialogues for common situations, such as introducing yourself, making a purchase, or making plans with a friend. Practice these dialogues out loud, focusing on fluidity and pronunciation.

Day 10: Listening and Speaking Practice

- **Listening Exercise:** Find resources such as songs, podcasts, or videos in Mexican Spanish. Listen carefully to catch pronunciation nuances, greetings, numbers, and the use of verbs in context. Try to transcribe or summarize what you hear.

- **Speaking Challenge:** Engage in a conversation in Spanish, focusing on the topics you've covered. This can be with a language exchange partner, tutor, or even practicing speaking to yourself in the mirror. The goal is to use as much of what you've learned as possible in a free-form conversation.

Additional Tips for Days 6-10:

- **Review Regularly:** Repetition is key to retention. Go over your notes from the previous days, and use flashcards if helpful.

- **Speak Aloud:** Always practice speaking out loud, even when reviewing written material. This will help solidify pronunciation and make you more comfortable using the language in conversations.

- **Be Patient and Positive:** Language learning is a process filled with progress and occasional setbacks. Celebrate your successes, and don't be discouraged by mistakes. They're a natural part of learning.

These five days of review and practical application are crucial for cementing the basics of Mexican Spanish. By actively engaging with the material, you're not just memorizing; you're starting to think and communicate in the language. Keep up the great work, and remember, every bit of practice brings you closer to fluency. ¡Buena suerte!

Part 2: Days 11-20 - Building Conversational Foundations

Day 11: Nouns, Articles, and Adjectives

Welcome to Day 11 of your journey into Mexican Spanish! Having mastered the basics, you're now ready to dive deeper into the language's structure. Today, we focus on nouns, articles, and adjectives—a trio that forms the backbone of descriptive language. Understanding how these elements work together will enhance your ability to describe people, places, things, and ideas, enriching your conversations significantly.

Nouns

Nouns are words that name people, places, things, or ideas. In Spanish, every noun has a gender, either masculine or feminine, which influences how it interacts with other words in a sentence.

- Masculine nouns often end in -o (e.g., **amigo** - friend), while feminine nouns typically end in -a (e.g., **casa** - house). There are exceptions, so it's important to learn the gender of nouns as you go.

Articles

Articles in Spanish agree in gender and number with the nouns they accompany. There are definite articles (the) and indefinite articles (a, an, some).

- Definite articles: **el** (masculine singular), **la** (feminine singular), **los** (masculine plural), **las** (feminine plural).

- Indefinite articles: **un** (masculine singular), **una** (feminine singular), **unos** (masculine plural), **unas** (feminine plural).

Adjectives

Adjectives describe nouns, providing details about size, quantity, color, opinion, and more. In Spanish, adjectives must agree with the nouns they describe in terms of gender and number.

- For example, **amigo** (friend) is masculine, so "good" is **bueno**: **un buen amigo**. For a feminine noun like **casa** (house), "good" becomes **buena**: **una buena casa**.

Putting It All Together

Combining nouns, articles, and adjectives allows you to form descriptive sentences. Remember, adjectives usually come after the noun in Spanish.

- **El gato negro** (The black cat)
- **Una ciudad hermosa** (A beautiful city)

Practice Exercise

1. Choose five nouns from a vocabulary list or your surroundings.
2. Determine their gender and write them down with both their definite and indefinite articles.
3. Add an adjective to each noun, ensuring agreement in gender and number.
4. Form complete sentences using these noun-adjective pairs, expressing likes or dislikes, presence or absence, etc.

Cultural Insight

Adjectives in Spanish often go beyond physical descriptions, touching on personality traits and emotions, which are highly valued in Mexican culture. Describing someone as **amable** (kind) or **trabajador** (hardworking) can reflect not just personal qualities but also social values.

Congratulations on completing Day 11! Today's lesson is a stepping stone toward expressing more complex ideas and engaging in richer conversations. Keep practicing these structures, and don't hesitate to expand your vocabulary with new nouns and adjectives. Tomorrow, we'll explore forming questions and answers, a crucial skill for interactive communication. ¡Hasta mañana!

Day 12: Forming Questions and Answers

Welcome to Day 12! Having built a solid foundation in nouns, articles, and adjectives, it's time to venture into the dynamic world of questions and answers. This essential skill will not only boost your interactive communication but also enhance your understanding of spoken Spanish. Today, you'll learn how to form basic questions and provide responses, enabling you to engage in conversations more actively.

The Structure of Questions

In Spanish, forming questions can be as simple as changing the intonation of a statement. For written Spanish, question marks are used at both the beginning (inverted) and the end of a question. Additionally, question words can be used to ask for specific information.

Basic Question Words:

- **¿Qué?** (What?) - Asking for information or clarification.

- **¿Quién?** (Who?) - Asking about people.

- **¿Dónde?** (Where?) - Asking about place or location.

- **¿Cuándo?** (When?) - Asking about time.

- **¿Por qué?** (Why?) - Asking for reasons.

- **¿Cómo?** (How?) - Asking about manner or condition.

- **¿Cuánto/a?** (How much?) - Asking about quantity or price (use **cuántos/as** for plural).

Forming Yes/No Questions

To form a yes/no question, you can simply raise the intonation at the end of a statement. Alternatively, you can use **¿Verdad?** (Right?) or **¿No?** at the end of a statement to turn it into a question.

- **Tienes un perro.** (You have a dog.) becomes **¿Tienes un perro?** (Do you have a dog?)

Providing Answers

Short answers in Spanish typically include the verb, either in the affirmative or negative form.

- **Sí, tengo un perro.** (Yes, I have a dog.)

- **No, no tengo un perro.** (No, I don't have a dog.)

Practice Exercise

1. **Create Questions:** Using the question words, form questions that you might use in everyday situations. For example, **¿Dónde está el baño?** (Where is the bathroom?)

2. **Formulate Responses:** Write answers to your questions, practicing both affirmative and negative forms.

Examples to Get You Started

- Q: **¿Qué hora es?** (What time is it?)

- A: **Son las tres.** (It's three o'clock.)

- Q: **¿Cómo estás hoy?** (How are you today?)

- A: **Estoy bien, gracias.** (I'm well, thank you.)

Cultural Insight

Asking questions is a fundamental part of engaging in conversations and shows interest in the other person and their culture. In Mexican culture, personal interactions often begin with questions about well-being, family, and food, reflecting the importance of personal connections and hospitality.

Congratulations on completing Day 12! Now that you can form basic questions and answers, you're equipped to take part in conversations more actively. Practice these structures with a friend or language partner, and try to incorporate them into your daily Spanish use. Tomorrow, we'll delve into everyday activities and routines, expanding your ability to talk about your day in Spanish. ¡Nos vemos!

Day 13: Everyday Activities and Routines

Welcome to Day 13! Today, we're going to enrich your conversational skills by focusing on how to talk about everyday activities and routines. This knowledge is not only fundamental for describing your own life but also for asking about others' daily habits, fostering deeper connections through shared experiences. By the end of this lesson, you'll be equipped to discuss what you do every day, from morning until night, in Mexican Spanish.

Vocabulary for Daily Activities

First, let's expand your vocabulary with verbs and phrases related to daily routines:

- **Despertarse** (to wake up)
- **Levantarse** (to get up)
- **Tomar un baño/ducharse** (to take a bath/shower)
- **Vestirse** (to get dressed)
- **Desayunar** (to have breakfast)
- **Ir al trabajo/escuela** (to go to work/school)
- **Trabajar** (to work)
- **Estudiar** (to study)
- **Almorzar** (to have lunch)

- **Regresar a casa** (to return home)
- **Cenar** (to have dinner)
- **Dormir** (to sleep)

Constructing Sentences about Daily Routines

To talk about your routines, you'll often use the first person singular form of verbs. Remember, many verbs related to routines are reflexive, indicating that the action is performed by and upon the subject. Here's how to conjugate reflexive verbs in the present tense:

- **Yo me despierto a las 7 a.m.** (I wake up at 7 a.m.)
- **Me baño antes de desayunar.** (I take a bath before breakfast.)

When discussing activities that aren't reflexive, simply use the appropriate verb conjugation:

- **Trabajo de 9 a 5.** (I work from 9 to 5.)
- **Estudio español por la noche.** (I study Spanish in the evening.)

Using Frequency Adverbs

To add detail to your routines, incorporate frequency adverbs:

- **Siempre** (always)
- **A menudo** (often)
- **A veces** (sometimes)
- **Raramente** (rarely)
- **Nunca** (never)

For example:

- **A menudo voy al gimnasio después del trabajo.** (I often go to the gym after work.)

Practice Exercise

1. Write down your daily routine using the new verbs and phrases you've learned. Start from when you wake up and go through to when you go to bed.

2. Try to include frequency adverbs to describe how often you perform each activity.

Cultural Insight

Discussing daily routines is a common way to find common ground with someone new. In Mexican culture, sharing aspects of your daily life can open doors to deeper conversations about family, work, and leisure, reflecting the communal nature of the society.

Congratulations on completing Day 13! You're now able to talk about daily activities and routines, a crucial step in using Spanish to describe your life and inquire about others'. Keep practicing these structures, and don't hesitate to add more activities and verbs as you learn them. Tomorrow, we'll look into describing people and places, further expanding your ability to engage in meaningful conversations. ¡Hasta mañana!

Day 14: Describing People and Places

On Day 14 of your journey into Mexican Spanish, we'll explore how to describe people and places. This skill is essential for sharing impressions, giving details about friends and family, and talking about locations you visit. Mastering descriptions will not only enhance your conversational abilities but also help you paint vivid pictures with your words, bringing your stories to life.

Descriptive Adjectives

To describe people and places, you'll need a set of adjectives that can capture qualities, characteristics, and physical appearances. Remember, in Spanish, adjectives must agree in gender (masculine or feminine) and number (singular or plural) with the nouns they describe.

Here are some adjectives to get you started:

- **Alto/a** (tall)
- **Bajo/a** (short)
- **Grande** (big)
- **Pequeño/a** (small)
- **Joven** (young)
- **Viejo/a** (old)
- **Bonito/a** (pretty, can also be used for places)

- **Feo/a** (ugly)

- **Amable** (kind)

- **Simpático/a** (nice)

Describing People

When describing people, focus on physical characteristics, personality traits, and emotional states. Use the verb **ser** for permanent traits (such as personality or physical characteristics) and **estar** for temporary states (such as feelings or conditions).

Examples:

- **Mi hermano es alto y simpático.** (My brother is tall and nice.)

- **Ella está feliz hoy.** (She is happy today.)

Describing Places

Describing places involves giving details about size, location, and general impressions. You might also want to talk about the activities that take place there.

Examples:

- **La playa es hermosa y tranquila.** (The beach is beautiful and peaceful.)

- **Este restaurante es pequeño pero acogedor.** (This restaurant is small but cozy.)

Using "Hay" for Descriptions

"Hay" translates to "there is" or "there are" and is useful for describing what exists or occurs in a particular place.

- **Hay muchas personas en el parque.** (There are many people in the park.)

- **Hay un río cerca de la ciudad.** (There is a river near the city.)

Practice Exercise

1. Choose a person you know well and write a brief description, including both physical traits and personality.

2. Describe a place you love visiting. Focus on sensory details: what you see, hear, and feel there.

Cultural Insight

In Mexican culture, descriptions often go beyond the surface, reflecting deeper qualities and emotions. When describing people, it's common to mention not just how someone looks but also their character and heart—qualities highly valued in Mexican society.

Congratulations on completing Day 14! You're now able to describe people and places in Spanish, adding depth and detail to your conversations. Practice by describing your surroundings or characters from a story or film. Tomorrow, we'll move on to ordering food and dining out, a practical skill for any Spanish speaker. ¡Nos vemos mañana!

Day 15: Ordering Food and Dining Out

Welcome to Day 15, where we'll dive into one of the most enjoyable aspects of language and culture: food. Today's focus is on ordering food and dining out, essential skills for anyone traveling to a Spanish-speaking country or enjoying the local Mexican cuisine. You'll learn how to navigate a menu, place your order, and handle common dining scenarios with ease.

Key Vocabulary for Dining Out

- **Menú** (menu)
- **Plato** (dish)
- **Bebida** (drink)
- **Entrada** (appetizer)
- **Plato principal** (main course)
- **Postre** (dessert)
- **Cuenta** (bill)
- **Mesero/a** (waiter/waitress)

Phrases for Ordering Food

To get started, here are some phrases that will come in handy:

- **¿Me puede traer el menú, por favor?** (Can you bring me the menu, please?)

- **Quisiera pedir...** (I would like to order...)
- **¿Cuál es la especialidad de la casa?** (What is the house specialty?)
- **¿Qué me recomienda?** (What do you recommend?)
- **Para mí, el/la...** (For me, the...)
- **¿Tiene platos vegetarianos?** (Do you have vegetarian dishes?)
- **Una mesa para dos, por favor.** (A table for two, please.)

Asking about Ingredients

If you have dietary restrictions or are curious about what's in a dish, use:

- **¿Lleva...?** (Does it contain...?)
- **Soy alérgico/a a...** (I'm allergic to...)
- **¿Puede hacerlo sin...?** (Can you make it without...?)

After the Meal

To conclude your dining experience gracefully, you might need:

- **La cuenta, por favor.** (The bill, please.)
- **¿Aceptan tarjetas?** (Do you accept cards?)
- **Estuvo delicioso.** (It was delicious.)

Practice Exercise

1. Create a dialogue between yourself and a waiter, from entering the restaurant to paying the bill. Include greetings, ordering, and asking for recommendations.

2. Write down what you would order using the phrases learned today, imagining you're at your favorite Mexican restaurant.

Cultural Insight

Dining out in Mexico is not just about the food; it's about the experience. Meals are often long and leisurely, seen as an opportunity to enjoy good company and conversation. Tipping is customary, usually around 10-15% of the bill, reflecting appreciation for the service.

Congratulations on completing Day 15! You now have the tools to navigate a dining experience in Spanish, from choosing your meal to expressing satisfaction with your food. These skills will not only serve you in restaurants but also help you bond over meals, a central part of Mexican culture and hospitality. Tomorrow, we'll explore how to navigate transportation and getting around, further enhancing your travel and conversational skills. ¡Buen provecho y hasta mañana!

Days 16-20: Conversational Foundations Review

Congratulations on reaching the midpoint of your journey to fluency in Mexican Spanish! Over the last few days, you've enriched your vocabulary and skills with essential knowledge for describing people and places, discussing daily routines, and navigating dining experiences. This review period is dedicated to reinforcing these concepts, correcting any areas of difficulty, and practicing your conversational skills in a variety of contexts.

Day 16: Review of Nouns, Articles, and Adjectives

- **Exercise:** Revisit the nouns, articles, and adjectives you've learned. Create descriptive sentences combining these elements, focusing on agreement in gender and number. For example, describe items in your room or office in Spanish.

- **Cultural Insight:** Pay attention to how adjectives can change meaning slightly depending on their placement before or after a noun. This nuance can add depth to your descriptions and conversations.

Day 17: Crafting Questions and Answers

- **Exercise:** Practice forming questions using the question words you've learned. Then, answer your questions, both affirmatively and negatively. Try to incorporate vocabulary from your descriptions of people, places, and daily routines.

- **Practical Application:** Engage in a mock conversation with a partner or record yourself, alternating between asking questions and answering them. Focus on using correct intonation for questions.

Day 18: Describing Daily Routines

- **Exercise:** Write a detailed account of your typical day or imagine a day in the life of someone else, using the verbs and expressions for daily activities. Include frequency adverbs to indicate how often you perform each activity.

- **Cultural Insight:** Reflect on how daily routines might differ in Mexico compared to your own country. Consider the typical times for meals, siesta traditions, and the importance of family time.

Day 19: Ordering Food and Dining Conversations

- **Exercise:** Create a detailed scenario of dining out, from entering the restaurant to paying the bill. Include dialogue with the server, questions about the menu, and comments on the food. Practice this scenario out loud, focusing on pronunciation and fluidity.

- **Practical Tip:** Review menu terms and dishes specific to Mexican cuisine. Understanding these will enhance your dining experiences and help you navigate menus with confidence.

Day 20: Comprehensive Conversation Practice

- **Exercise:** Combine all the elements you've reviewed into a comprehensive conversation. This could be a role-play scenario that includes meeting someone new, discussing your daily routines, describing your family or home, and inviting them to dine out.

- **Challenge:** Try to incorporate some cultural insights or ask questions that would lead to a discussion about cultural differences and similarities.

Additional Tips for Days 16-20:

- **Active Listening:** Incorporate listening exercises using Spanish podcasts, music, or videos. Focus on identifying the vocabulary and structures you've learned.

- **Speak, Speak, Speak:** The key to solidifying your conversational skills is practice. Don't be afraid to make mistakes; use them as learning opportunities.

- **Seek Feedback:** If possible, get feedback from native speakers or language exchange partners. They can offer invaluable insights into your pronunciation, grammar, and usage.

These five days of review are crucial for cementing the conversational foundations you've built. By actively engaging with the exercises and seeking opportunities to use what you've learned, you're making significant strides toward fluency in Mexican Spanish. Keep up the great work, and remember, every conversation is a step forward in your language learning journey. ¡Buena suerte y hasta la próxima!

Part 3: Days 21-30 - Navigating Daily Situations

Day 21: Directions, Transportation, and Getting Around

Today, on Day 21, we embark on a practical exploration of getting around in a Spanish-speaking environment. Mastering directions, transportation terms, and the nuances of navigating spaces is crucial for anyone planning to travel or live in a Spanish-speaking country. This lesson will equip you with the language skills needed to ask for directions, understand instructions, and discuss various modes of transportation.

Vocabulary for Directions and Transportation

First, let's expand your vocabulary with essential terms related to directions and transportation:

- **Dirección** (direction)
- **Izquierda** (left)
- **Derecha** (right)
- **Recto/ahead** (straight)
- **Esquina** (corner)
- **Semáforo** (traffic light)
- **Parada de autobús** (bus stop)
- **Estación de metro** (subway station)

- **Tren** (train)
- **Taxi** (taxi)
- **Aeropuerto** (airport)

Phrases for Asking and Giving Directions

Being able to ask for and understand directions is invaluable. Here are some phrases to help:

- **¿Dónde está...?** (Where is...?)
- **¿Cómo llego a...?** (How do I get to...?)
- **Ve/Vaya a la izquierda/derecha.** (Go to the left/right.)
- **Sigue/Siga recto.** (Continue straight.)
- **Está a la vuelta de la esquina.** (It's around the corner.)

Discussing Transportation

When discussing or inquiring about modes of transportation, these phrases will come in handy:

- **¿Cuál es el autobús/metro para...?** (Which is the bus/subway for...?)
- **¿A qué hora sale el tren?** (What time does the train leave?)
- **¿Dónde puedo tomar un taxi?** (Where can I get a taxi?)

Practice Exercise

1. Imagine you're visiting a Spanish-speaking city. Write a short dialogue where you ask a local for directions to three different

places: a hotel, a restaurant, and a museum. Include questions about the nearest bus stop or subway station.

2. Describe a journey from your current location to a place you frequently visit, using the vocabulary for directions and transportation. Try to be as detailed as possible.

Cultural Insight

In many Spanish-speaking countries, giving directions is often an exercise in creativity. Locals might use landmarks, buildings, or other points of interest rather than street names or numbers. It's also common for directions to be somewhat approximate, so asking multiple people for directions to the same place can be helpful.

Congratulations on completing Day 21! You've taken a significant step toward independence in Spanish-speaking environments by learning how to navigate directions and transportation. These skills not only enhance your ability to move around but also deepen your engagement with the local culture and community. Tomorrow, we'll explore how to shop and transact in Spanish, further building your practical language skills. ¡Hasta mañana!

Day 22: Shopping and Transactions

Welcome to Day 22, where we'll delve into the language of shopping and transactions, an essential aspect of daily life and an invaluable skill while traveling or living in Spanish-speaking countries. Today's lesson will equip you with the phrases and vocabulary needed to navigate markets, stores, and various purchasing scenarios with confidence.

Key Vocabulary for Shopping

- **Tienda** (store)
- **Mercado** (market)
- **Precio** (price)
- **Dinero** (money)
- **Tarjeta de crédito** (credit card)
- **Efectivo** (cash)
- **Cambio** (change, as in money)
- **Recibo** (receipt)
- **Vendedor(a)** (salesperson)
- **Cliente** (customer)

Phrases for Shopping and Transactions

To engage in transactions and communicate effectively while shopping, familiarize yourself with these useful phrases:

- **¿Cuánto cuesta esto?** (How much does this cost?)
- **¿Tiene esto en otra talla/color?** (Do you have this in another size/color?)
- **Estoy buscando...** (I'm looking for...)
- **¿Puedo pagar con tarjeta?** (Can I pay with a card?)
- **¿Me puede dar un recibo, por favor?** (Can I have a receipt, please?)
- **Quisiera devolver esto.** (I would like to return this.)

Bargaining

In many markets and some stores, bargaining is common. Here are phrases that can help you negotiate a better price:

- **¿Tiene descuento?** (Is there a discount?)
- **Es muy caro. ¿Puede bajar el precio?** (It's very expensive. Can you lower the price?)
- **Le doy... por esto.** (I'll give you... for this.)

Practice Exercise

1. Create a dialogue between yourself and a vendor where you're buying souvenirs from a local market. Include asking for the price, negotiating, and making the purchase.

2. Write a scenario where you're shopping for clothes, including asking for different sizes, inquiring about the price, and completing the transaction.

Cultural Insight

Shopping in Spanish-speaking countries can be a vibrant and interactive experience, especially in local markets. It's not only about making a purchase but also about social interaction and cultural exchange. Politeness and a friendly demeanor go a long way, and a few words in Spanish can significantly enrich the experience. Remember, bargaining is often expected in markets but should be done respectfully.

Congratulations on completing Day 22! You're now well-equipped to handle shopping and transactions in Spanish, from asking about prices to negotiating a deal. These practical skills will enhance your travels and everyday life, offering ample opportunities to practice Spanish in real-world situations. Tomorrow, we'll explore making plans and extending invitations, further broadening your conversational abilities. ¡Hasta entonces!

DAY 23: MAKING PLANS AND APPOINTMENTS

Today, on Day 23, we delve into making plans and scheduling appointments, an essential aspect of communication that helps us navigate social and professional life in Spanish-speaking environments. Whether it's catching up with friends, setting up a meeting, or booking a service, the ability to articulate plans clearly is key. Let's enhance your conversational toolkit with the necessary phrases and structures.

Essential Vocabulary

- **Plan** (plan)

- **Cita** (appointment or date)

- **Reunión** (meeting)

- **Evento** (event)

- **Agenda** (schedule)

- **Disponible** (available)

- **Ocupado/a** (busy)

- **Confirmar** (to confirm)

- **Cancelar** (to cancel)

- **Mover / Posponer** (to move / to postpone)

Phrases for Making Plans and Appointments

- **¿Estás libre el...?** (Are you free on...?)
- **¿Podemos reunirnos el...?** (Can we meet on...?)
- **Necesito hacer una cita para...** (I need to make an appointment for...)
- **¿A qué hora te viene bien?** (What time is good for you?)
- **Estoy disponible a las...** (I am available at...)
- **¿Puedes confirmar...?** (Can you confirm...?)
- **Tengo que cancelar nuestra cita.** (I have to cancel our appointment.)
- **¿Podemos moverlo a...?** (Can we move it to...?)

Scheduling Social Activities

Social interactions often require flexibility and the ability to suggest alternatives. Here's how you can navigate these conversations:

- **¿Te gustaría ir a...?** (Would you like to go to...?)
- **Me encantaría, pero estoy ocupado/a. ¿Qué tal el...?** (I would love to, but I'm busy. How about on...?)

Practice Exercise

1. Imagine you're planning a weekend trip with friends. Write a dialogue that includes suggesting the trip, discussing availability, and agreeing on the details.

2. Script a scenario where you need to book a doctor's appointment over the phone. Include providing your availability, asking about the doctor's availability, and confirming the appointment.

Cultural Insight

In many Spanish-speaking cultures, personal relationships are highly valued, and making plans often involves a considerate exchange. It's common for plans to be made somewhat last minute or for schedules to change. Flexibility and patience are appreciated qualities. Additionally, confirming plans a day before or the day of is a common practice, ensuring that everyone is still available as discussed.

Congratulations on completing Day 23! You're now equipped to make plans, schedule appointments, and handle the adjustments that often come with social and professional engagements in Spanish. These skills not only aid in logistical organization but also open up new avenues for deepening relationships and understanding cultural nuances. Tomorrow, we'll tackle expressing likes, dislikes, and preferences, further enriching your conversational repertoire. ¡Nos vemos mañana!

Day 24: Expressing Likes, Dislikes, and Preferences

Welcome to Day 24, where we focus on expressing likes, dislikes, and preferences. This ability is central to sharing more about yourself and engaging in deeper conversations. Whether discussing food, activities, music, or any other interest, conveying what you enjoy or don't enjoy helps build connections and understandings. Let's dive into the language patterns that will enable you to express your preferences clearly and learn about others' as well.

Key Verbs and Expressions

- **Gustar** (to like) – Unlike the direct English equivalent, "gustar" functions differently, indicating that something pleases someone. It's often used with indirect object pronouns.

- **Encantar** (to love, used like "gustar" to indicate enjoyment or delight)

- **Preferir** (to prefer)

- **Interesar** (to be interested in)

Structure with "Gustar" and Similar Verbs

Remember, when using "gustar" and verbs like it, the thing liked is the subject, and the person who likes it is indicated by an indirect object pronoun.

- **Me gusta la pizza.** (I like pizza.)

- **Nos encanta viajar.** (We love traveling.)
- **Le interesan los libros.** (He/She is interested in books.)

Expressing Dislikes

To express dislikes, you simply place "no" before the indirect object pronoun.

- **No me gusta correr.** (I don't like running.)
- **A ellos no les encanta la música clásica.** (They don't love classical music.)

Discussing Preferences

To talk about preferences, use the verb "preferir," which is a stem-changing verb (e-ie).

- **Prefiero el té al café.** (I prefer tea over coffee.)
- **Ella prefiere estudiar por la noche.** (She prefers to study at night.)

Practice Exercise

1. Write five sentences about things you like using "gustar" and "encantar."

2. Write five sentences about things you don't like.

3. Describe your preferences in various scenarios, like choosing food at a restaurant, selecting a movie to watch, or planning weekend activities.

Cultural Insight

Expressing likes and dislikes is often a starting point for many conversations and is crucial in social settings. In Spanish-speaking cultures, sharing and respecting personal preferences is seen as part of getting to know someone better. However, it's common to phrase dislikes politely to maintain harmony and respect within conversations.

Congratulations on completing Day 24! You can now share and inquire about likes, dislikes, and preferences, opening up a world of conversation topics. This skill is not just about expressing opinions but also about fostering connections and showing interest in others' passions. Tomorrow, we'll explore handling emergencies and unexpected situations, further preparing you for a wide range of conversational contexts. ¡Hasta mañana!

Day 25: Cultural Norms and Social Etiquette

Welcome to Day 25, a day dedicated to understanding and navigating the cultural norms and social etiquette of Spanish-speaking societies. Grasping these unwritten rules is as crucial as mastering the language itself, as they inform respectful and meaningful interactions. Today, we'll explore key aspects of social conduct, common courtesies, and cultural sensitivities that will enrich your communication and enhance your cultural awareness.

Greetings and Goodbyes

- **Personal Space:** In Spanish-speaking cultures, personal space may be closer than what you're accustomed to. Greetings often involve a handshake, a light hug, or kisses on the cheek (one or two, depending on the country).

- **Formality:** Use "usted" in formal situations or when addressing elders, and "tú" with friends, children, or peers. Pay attention to how others refer to you and reciprocate accordingly.

Dining Etiquette

- **Meal Times:** Meal times can differ significantly. Lunch is typically the main meal and may occur later than you expect, often between 2 and 4 PM, while dinner can be as late as 9 PM or beyond.

- **Table Manners:** It's customary to say "buen provecho" before starting to eat, similar to "bon appétit." Wait for your host or the eldest person at the table to start eating.

Social Gatherings

- **Punctuality:** Arriving a bit late to social gatherings is often acceptable and sometimes expected. However, for business or formal appointments, punctuality is respected.
- **Invitations:** If invited to someone's home, bringing a small gift like flowers, wine, or sweets is a thoughtful gesture.

Respectful Interactions

- **Titles and Names:** Using titles such as "Señor" (Mr.), "Señora" (Mrs.), or "Señorita" (Miss) followed by the surname shows respect. Wait to be invited to use first names.
- **Listening and Speaking:** Interrupting or raising your voice can be seen as disrespectful. It's important to listen attentively and speak politely.

Navigating Conversations

- **Avoiding Stereotypes:** Be mindful of avoiding stereotypes or making assumptions based on nationality. Show interest in learning from individuals about their unique experiences and perspectives.
- **Sensitive Topics:** Exercise caution when discussing politics, religion, and other potentially sensitive topics. If such subjects arise, listen respectfully and share your views thoughtfully, if at all.

Practice Exercise

1. Reflect on the cultural norms and social etiquette mentioned. Write a short paragraph on how understanding these norms might

change or enhance your approach to speaking Spanish and interacting in Spanish-speaking countries.

2. Create a dialogue that includes a social situation, such as a dinner invitation or meeting someone new, incorporating the etiquette and norms discussed.

Cultural Insight

Understanding and respecting cultural norms and social etiquette not only facilitates smoother interactions but also deepens connections with Spanish speakers. It reflects an appreciation for the rich tapestry of traditions, values, and behaviors that define a culture. As you continue to learn Spanish, integrating these insights into your interactions will make your communication more authentic and rewarding.

Congratulations on completing Day 25! By now, you have a deeper appreciation of the cultural nuances that accompany the Spanish language. Such knowledge not only enhances your linguistic abilities but also enriches your cultural competence, paving the way for more meaningful and respectful interactions. Tomorrow, we'll delve into the realm of health, wellness, and navigating medical situations in Spanish. ¡Hasta entonces!

DAYS 26-30: DAILY SITUATIONS REVIEW AND PRACTICE

As we reach the final stretch of Part 3, these next five days are dedicated to reviewing and practicing everything we've covered about navigating daily situations. From asking for directions and shopping to making plans and understanding cultural norms, you've gained valuable skills that prepare you for real-life interactions in Spanish-speaking environments. This review period aims to solidify these skills, correct any misunderstandings, and increase your confidence in using Spanish in a variety of contexts.

Day 26: Review of Directions and Transportation

- **Exercise:** Create a detailed guide for a friend visiting a Spanish-speaking country, including directions from the airport to a hotel, using public transportation, and getting to three must-see places in the city.

- **Challenge:** Try to recall all transportation-related vocabulary and phrases without referring back to the lesson. Then, check your accuracy and review any missed or forgotten terms.

Day 27: Shopping and Transactions Deep Dive

- **Exercise:** Simulate a shopping experience, either by visiting a local store where Spanish is spoken or through an online shopping simulation in Spanish. Focus on asking about prices, negotiating, and making purchases.

- **Reflection:** Write about your simulated shopping experience, detailing the conversations you had or would have had. Identify any areas for improvement in vocabulary or confidence.

Day 28: Revisiting Plans, Appointments, and Social Etiquette

- **Exercise:** Plan an entire week in Spanish, including social outings, appointments, and personal time. Use the calendar terms, days of the week, and expressions for making plans and appointments that you've learned.

- **Discussion:** With a partner or in a study group, discuss your planned week. Ask about and provide suggestions for each other's schedules, practicing giving and receiving advice and opinions.

Day 29: Expressing Likes, Dislikes, and Cultural Insights

- **Exercise:** Create a presentation or write a short essay about your favorite aspects of Spanish-speaking cultures, including cuisine, traditions, or any personal experiences. Use the language patterns for expressing likes, dislikes, and preferences.

- **Cultural Exchange:** Share your presentation or essay with peers or on a language learning platform. Invite feedback on both your language use and the content of your cultural insights.

Day 30: Comprehensive Practice Through Role-Play

- **Role-Play Scenarios:** In groups or with a partner, engage in role-play scenarios that incorporate elements from all the daily situations covered. Scenarios might include getting lost and asking for directions, hosting a dinner party, attending a social event, or a day out shopping.

- **Feedback Session:** After each role-play, provide and receive feedback focusing on language accuracy, cultural appropriateness, and fluency. Discuss any challenges encountered and how they might be overcome in future interactions.

Additional Tips for Days 26-30:

- **Immersive Listening:** Enhance your review by listening to Spanish podcasts, watching movies, or engaging with music that includes themes from the daily situations covered. Note any new vocabulary or expressions.

- **Daily Language Journal:** Keep a journal of your interactions or observations related to the daily situations discussed. Note down new words, phrases, or cultural insights you encounter.

- **Language Exchange:** If possible, participate in a language exchange focused on discussing daily life and cultural experiences. Use the opportunity to practice and refine your conversational skills.

Congratulations on completing the review and practice days of Part 3! You've worked hard to enhance your ability to navigate a wide range of daily situations in Spanish. These foundational skills not only boost your linguistic competence but also deepen your cultural understanding, making your interactions more meaningful and rewarding. Keep practicing, stay curious, and continue to explore the rich tapestry of Spanish-speaking cultures. ¡Adelante y buena suerte!

Part 4: Days 31-40 - Exploring Grammar and Structure

Day 31: Introduction to Tenses: Present, Past, and Future

Welcome to Day 31, where we embark on a crucial aspect of language learning: understanding verb tenses. Today's lesson introduces the present, past, and future tenses in Spanish, laying the groundwork for expressing actions across different time frames. This foundational knowledge will significantly enhance your ability to discuss past events, describe current situations, and talk about future plans.

The Present Tense

You've already been using the present tense to talk about preferences, routines, and daily activities. The present tense in Spanish is used to describe current actions, habitual activities, and general truths.

- **Hablar** (to speak):
    - Yo hablo (I speak)
    - Tú hablas (You speak)
    - Él/Ella/Usted habla (He/She/You formal speak)
- **Comer** (to eat):
    - Yo como (I eat)
    - Tú comes (You eat)

- Él/Ella/Usted come (He/She/You formal eat)
- **Vivir** (to live):
  - Yo vivo (I live)
  - Tú vives (You live)
  - Él/Ella/Usted vive (He/She/You formal live)

The Past Tense

Spanish has two simple past tenses: the preterite and the imperfect. Today, we'll focus on the preterite, which is used to describe actions that were completed in the past.

- **Hablar** in the preterite:
  - Yo hablé (I spoke)
  - Tú hablaste (You spoke)
  - Él/Ella/Usted habló (He/She/You formal spoke)
- **Comer** in the preterite:
  - Yo comí (I ate)
  - Tú comiste (You ate)
  - Él/Ella/Usted comió (He/She/You formal ate)

The Future Tense

The future tense in Spanish is relatively straightforward and is used to talk about actions that will happen in the future. It can also express wonder or uncertainty about the present.

- **Hablar** in the future:
  - Yo hablaré (I will speak)
  - Tú hablarás (You will speak)
  - Él/Ella/Usted hablará (He/She/You formal will speak)
- **Comer** in the future:
  - Yo comeré (I will eat)
  - Tú comerás (You will eat)
  - Él/Ella/Usted comerá (He/She/You formal will eat)

Practice Exercise

1. Choose five verbs and conjugate them in the present, past (preterite), and future tenses for "yo" (I) and "tú" (you) forms.
2. Write three sentences for each tense, using different verbs to describe actions. For example:
   - Present: **Yo estudio español todos los días.** (I study Spanish every day.)
   - Past: **Ayer hablé con mi amigo.** (Yesterday, I spoke with my friend.)
   - Future: **Mañana comeremos paella.** (Tomorrow, we will eat paella.)

Cultural Insight

Understanding and using verb tenses correctly can provide insights into the storytelling traditions of Spanish-speaking cultures. Narratives, whether in oral or written form, often weave through different time frames, reflecting the rich history and diverse experiences of these cultures.

Congratulations on completing Day 31! Today's introduction to verb tenses is a significant milestone in your language learning journey. Mastery of these tenses will open up new avenues for expressing thoughts and experiences more accurately. Keep practicing, and soon you'll be comfortable discussing events across any time frame in Spanish. Tomorrow, we'll dive deeper into the past tense, exploring nuances and uses. ¡Hasta mañana!

DAY 32: MODAL VERBS AND USEFUL EXPRESSIONS

On Day 32, we explore the world of modal verbs and useful expressions in Spanish. Modal verbs are auxiliary verbs that modify the main verb to express necessity, ability, permission, or possibility. These verbs are pivotal for nuanced communication, allowing you to articulate intentions, capabilities, and more. Today's lesson will equip you with these versatile tools to enhance your conversational fluency.

Key Modal Verbs in Spanish

- **Poder** (to be able to/can)

- **Deber** (must/should, indicating obligation or probability)

- **Querer** (to want)

- **Tener que** (to have to, expressing necessity)

- **Soler** (to usually do something)

Using Modal Verbs

Modal verbs are used alongside the infinitive form of the main verb. Here's how to conjugate and use some of the most common modal verbs:

- **Poder:**
  - Yo puedo hablar español. (I can speak Spanish.)
  - Puedes venir mañana? (Can you come tomorrow?)

- **Deber:**
  - Debes ver esa película. (You should see that movie.)
  - Él debe estar en casa. (He must be at home.)
- **Querer:**
  - Quiero aprender a bailar. (I want to learn to dance.)
  - ¿Quieres más café? (Do you want more coffee?)
- **Tener que:**
  - Tengo que estudiar para el examen. (I have to study for the exam.)
  - Tenemos que irnos ahora. (We have to go now.)
- **Soler:**
  - Suelo viajar en verano. (I usually travel in the summer.)
  - ¿Sueles desayunar temprano? (Do you usually have breakfast early?)

Useful Expressions with Modal Verbs

Incorporating modal verbs into your conversations allows for expressing more complex ideas. Here are some expressions that you might find useful:

- **No poder esperar** (to can't wait)
  - No puedo esperar para verte. (I can't wait to see you.)
- **Tener que ver con** (to have to do with)

- Esto tiene que ver con lo que dijiste ayer. (This has to do with what you said yesterday.)

Practice Exercise

1. Conjugate each modal verb in the first person singular (yo) and second person singular (tú) forms.

2. Create sentences using each modal verb. Try to cover a variety of contexts, such as obligations, desires, abilities, and habits.

3. Formulate questions using modal verbs, aiming to practice both asking and answering.

Cultural Insight

Modal verbs are often softened with phrases to make requests or suggestions more polite, reflecting the importance of courtesy in Spanish-speaking cultures. For instance, "¿Podrías pasarme la sal?" is a softer, more polite way of asking, "Could you pass me the salt?" than using "puedes."

Congratulations on completing Day 32! You've now added an essential layer of sophistication to your Spanish through the understanding and use of modal verbs. These verbs are crucial for expressing a wide range of meanings, from obligations and desires to capabilities and habits. As you continue to practice, try to incorporate these modal verbs into your daily conversations, enhancing both your fluency and your ability to engage in more complex interactions. Tomorrow, we'll tackle the imperative mood, further expanding your command of Spanish grammar. ¡Hasta mañana!

Day 33: The Imperative Mood and Giving Commands

Welcome to Day 33 of our Spanish language journey. Today, we're diving into the imperative mood, which is used to give commands, make requests, or offer advice. Understanding the imperative is essential for direct communication, instructing others, or simply telling a friend to relax and enjoy the moment. Let's explore how to form and use the imperative mood in Spanish.

Forming the Imperative

The imperative mood has different forms for affirmative and negative commands, and it varies depending on whether you're addressing someone in the tú (informal you), usted (formal you), nosotros (we), or vosotros (you all, informal, used in Spain) form.

Affirmative Commands

- **Tú:** For most verbs, use the third person singular (él, ella, usted) form of the present indicative. For example, "habla" (speak), "come" (eat), "vive" (live).

- **Usted:** Use the present subjunctive form. For example, "hable" (speak), "coma" (eat), "viva" (live).

- **Nosotros:** Use the present subjunctive form. For example, "hablemos" (let's speak), "comamos" (let's eat), "vivamos" (let's live).

- **Vosotros:** Add "d" to the infinitive for -ar verbs and replace the final -r of -er/-ir verbs with "d." For example, "hablad" (speak), "comed" (eat), "vivid" (live).

Negative Commands

For negative commands, use the tú, usted, nosotros, and vosotros forms of the present subjunctive.

- **Tú:** No hables (Don't speak), no comas (Don't eat), no vivas (Don't live).

- **Usted:** No hable, no coma, no viva.

- **Nosotros:** No hablemos, no comamos, no vivamos.

- **Vosotros:** No habléis, no comáis, no viváis.

Irregular Verbs

Some verbs have irregular affirmative tú commands, like "ser" (sé), "ir" (ve), "tener" (ten), and "venir" (ven).

Using the Imperative

- To give friendly advice or instructions, pair commands with "por favor" to soften the tone. For example, "Pasa, por favor" (Come in, please).

- Use reflexive verbs to give commands that involve the listener performing an action on themselves. Attach the reflexive pronoun to the end of affirmative commands. For example, "Siéntate" (Sit down).

Practice Exercise

1. Create a list of five daily activities. Write affirmative and negative commands for each activity using tú, usted, and nosotros forms.

2. Imagine you're organizing a group activity. Write a set of instructions using the imperative form, including both what to do and what not to do.

Cultural Insight

The use of the imperative mood in Spanish-speaking cultures requires sensitivity to context and tone. While giving commands is straightforward, the relationship between the speaker and listener, the situation, and the inclusion of "por favor" can significantly affect how the message is received. Being polite and respectful when issuing commands ensures positive interactions.

Congratulations on completing Day 33! You've now mastered the basics of giving commands and making requests in Spanish. The imperative mood is a powerful tool for direct communication, allowing you to engage more actively in Spanish-speaking environments. Practice using the imperative in everyday situations to become more comfortable with its forms and uses. Tomorrow, we'll delve into adverbs and frequency, further enhancing your ability to describe actions and situations. ¡Hasta mañana!

Day 34: Adverbs and Frequency

Welcome to Day 34, where we'll focus on adverbs, particularly those that indicate frequency. Adverbs are incredibly versatile and can modify verbs, adjectives, or other adverbs, providing additional information about how, when, where, and to what extent an action is performed. Today, we'll concentrate on adverbs that help us express how often actions occur, enhancing your ability to talk about habits, routines, and preferences.

Understanding Adverbs of Frequency

Adverbs of frequency tell us how often something happens. They're crucial for describing daily routines, habitual activities, and even exceptions to regular patterns.

Here are some common adverbs of frequency in Spanish, from most frequent to least frequent:

- **Siempre** (always)
- **Casi siempre** (almost always)
- **Frecuentemente / A menudo** (frequently / often)
- **Muchas veces** (many times)
- **A veces / Algunas veces** (sometimes)
- **Raramente / Rara vez** (rarely)
- **Casi nunca** (almost never)

- **Nunca** (never)

Placement of Adverbs

The placement of adverbs of frequency in a sentence can vary, but they're often found either before the main verb or between the auxiliary verb and the main verb in compound tenses.

- **Siempre estudio después de clase.** (I always study after class.)
- **He casi nunca comido sushi.** (I have almost never eaten sushi.)

Expressing Frequency with "Cuántas Veces"

When asking about the frequency of an action, you can use **"¿Cuántas veces...?"** (How many times...?).

- **¿Cuántas veces vas al gimnasio a la semana?** (How many times do you go to the gym in a week?)

Practice Exercise

1. Think about your typical week and write sentences describing your activities using adverbs of frequency. For example, "A menudo voy al cine los viernes." (I often go to the cinema on Fridays.)

2. Create questions about someone else's habits using **"¿Cuántas veces...?"** and try to answer those questions from your perspective or imagine the answers.

Using Adverbs to Modify Adjectives and Other Adverbs

Adverbs can also modify adjectives and other adverbs, adding depth to descriptions. **"Muy"** (very) and **"bastante"** (quite) are commonly used for this purpose.

- **Ella es muy inteligente.** (She is very intelligent.)

- **Hablamos bastante frecuentemente.** (We talk quite frequently.)

Cultural Insight

Discussing habits and routines is a common way to find common ground in conversations. In many Spanish-speaking cultures, sharing details about one's daily life, especially as it relates to family and social activities, is a way to build rapport. The use of adverbs of frequency can also reveal cultural patterns, such as the typical time for meals or social gatherings, which may vary significantly from one country to another.

Congratulations on completing Day 34! Today, you've gained valuable tools for describing how often activities occur, enhancing your ability to share about your life and inquire about others' in a more detailed and engaging way. Tomorrow, we'll explore adverbs and prepositions, further enriching your ability to express actions and relationships between elements in a sentence. ¡Hasta mañana!

Day 35: Prepositions and Location

Welcome to Day 35 of our journey into Spanish grammar and structure. Today, we're focusing on prepositions, particularly those related to location. Prepositions are small but mighty words that connect nouns, pronouns, or phrases to other words in a sentence, indicating relationships of place, time, direction, and more. Understanding how to use prepositions of location will significantly enhance your ability to describe where things are, give directions, and navigate your surroundings.

Key Prepositions of Location

- **En** (in, on, at) – Used for general locations. *Estoy en la biblioteca.* (I am in the library.)

- **A** (to, at) – Indicates direction or proximity. *Voy a la casa.* (I am going to the house.)

- **Cerca de** (near) – Indicates proximity. *La cafetería está cerca del parque.* (The café is near the park.)

- **Lejos de** (far from) – Indicates distance. *El aeropuerto está lejos de la ciudad.* (The airport is far from the city.)

- **Al lado de** (next to, beside) – Indicates adjacency. *La farmacia está al lado del banco.* (The pharmacy is next to the bank.)

- **Entre** (between) – Indicates something is in the middle of two points. *Mi casa está entre el supermercado y la escuela.* (My house is between the supermarket and the school.)

- **Delante de** (in front of) – Indicates something is before something else in space. *Hay un coche delante de la tienda.* (There is a car in front of the store.)

- **Detrás de** (behind) – Indicates something is at the back of something else. *El jardín está detrás de la casa.* (The garden is behind the house.)

- **Debajo de** (underneath, below) – Indicates a lower position. *El gato está debajo de la mesa.* (The cat is under the table.)

- **Encima de** (on top of, above) – Indicates a higher position. *Los libros están encima del escritorio.* (The books are on top of the desk.)

Using Prepositions in Sentences

Prepositions of location are frequently used to give directions, describe the layout of spaces, and talk about one's environment. They can be combined with verbs like *estar* (to be) to describe locations or with verbs of movement like *ir* (to go) to talk about direction.

Practice Exercise

1. Draw a simple map of a room or a neighborhood and label various objects or places.

2. Using your map, write sentences describing the location of each item or place relative to others. For example, "El parque está cerca de mi casa."

3. Create a short paragraph giving directions from one place to another using the prepositions you've learned.

Cultural Insight

Spatial orientation can reflect cultural aspects, such as the importance of certain places within a community. In many Spanish-speaking areas, landmarks rather than street names are often used to give directions. This highlights the relational and communal nature of navigating spaces, where understanding local landmarks and their significance becomes part of the cultural immersion.

Congratulations on completing Day 35! You now have a solid grasp of using prepositions to talk about location, an essential skill for describing environments, giving directions, and understanding descriptions of places. These tools not only aid in navigation but also in connecting more deeply with the cultural landscapes of Spanish-speaking regions. Tomorrow, we'll delve into combining verbs with prepositions to express various actions and relationships. ¡Hasta mañana!

Days 36-40: Grammar Deep Dive Review

As we approach the conclusion of this segment on exploring grammar and structure, the next five days are dedicated to reviewing, reinforcing, and practicing the concepts we've covered. From the introduction to tenses and modal verbs to the imperative mood, adverbs, prepositions, and location, you've gained valuable tools to enhance your grammatical accuracy and expressive capacity in Spanish. This review period aims to solidify your understanding, correct any misunderstandings, and boost your confidence in applying these structures in various contexts.

Day 36: Review of Tenses

- **Exercise:** Create a timeline of your typical day, including past, present, and future activities. Write sentences for each activity using the appropriate tense. For example, "Ayer trabajé hasta tarde" (Yesterday, I worked late), "Hoy trabajo desde casa" (Today, I'm working from home), "Mañana trabajaré en un proyecto nuevo" (Tomorrow, I will work on a new project).

- **Challenge:** Try to include at least one irregular verb in each tense.

Day 37: Modal Verbs and Useful Expressions

- **Exercise:** Write a short story or dialogue that incorporates modal verbs to express abilities, obligations, desires, and advice. For instance, "Debo estudiar para mi examen, pero quiero salir con mis amigos."

- **Reflection:** Consider how changing a modal verb alters the meaning of a sentence and your perception of the speaker's intent.

Day 38: The Imperative Mood

- **Exercise:** Imagine you're writing a recipe or a set of instructions for a game in Spanish. Use the imperative mood to direct your readers clearly. Remember to include both positive and negative commands.

- **Practice with Peers:** Share your instructions with classmates or language exchange partners. Ask for feedback on your use of the imperative mood and clarity of instructions.

Day 39: Adverbs and Frequency

- **Exercise:** Keep a diary entry in Spanish, describing your activities throughout the day with an emphasis on frequency. Use adverbs to detail how often you perform each activity and your feelings about them.

- **Discussion:** Share your diary entry with a study group or teacher. Discuss how adverbs of frequency can influence the perception of your habits and routines.

Day 40: Prepositions and Location

- **Exercise:** Describe a place that is important to you, such as your hometown or a favorite vacation spot, using prepositions of location to detail its features and the location of significant landmarks.

- **Interactive Activity:** Create a virtual tour of your described place using the prepositions of location. You could do this through a series of written descriptions, a recorded speech, or a visual presentation.

Additional Tips for Days 36-40:

- **Revisit and Reflect:** Go back to the exercises and notes from the past days. Identify any areas that are still challenging and set aside time for focused review.

- **Practice in Context:** Try to use the grammatical structures you're reviewing in real-life situations or through creative writing. Contextual practice helps cement your understanding.

- **Engage in Conversations:** Use language exchange opportunities to practice speaking. Focus on incorporating the grammatical structures you've reviewed, and don't hesitate to ask for corrections or explanations.

- **Use Technology:** Language learning apps and online exercises can provide additional practice and reinforcement, especially for verb conjugations and sentence structure.

Congratulations on completing the grammar deep dive review! You've worked diligently to strengthen your understanding of key grammatical structures, which are vital for effective communication in Spanish. These foundational skills will support your continued learning and mastery of the language. Keep practicing, remain curious, and embrace opportunities to use Spanish in your daily life. ¡Adelante y buena suerte!

PART 5: DAYS 41-50 - DEEPENING VOCABULARY AND USAGE

Day 41: Family and Relationships

Welcome to Day 41, where we turn our focus to expanding our vocabulary related to family and relationships. This area of language learning is particularly enriching, allowing us to talk about those closest to us and describe the nature of various relationships. Understanding and using these terms will enable you to share more about your personal life, ask others about their families, and navigate conversations about human connections in Spanish.

Key Vocabulary: Family Members

- **La familia** (The family)

- **Los padres** (Parents)

- **La madre** (Mother)

- **El padre** (Father)

- **Los hijos** (Children)

- **El hijo / La hija** (Son / Daughter)

- **Los hermanos** (Siblings)

- **El hermano / La hermana** (Brother / Sister)

- **Los abuelos** (Grandparents)

- **El abuelo / La abuela** (Grandfather / Grandmother)

- **Los nietos** (Grandchildren)

- **El nieto / La nieta** (Grandson / Granddaughter)
- **El tío / La tía** (Uncle / Aunt)
- **El primo / La prima** (Cousin)

Vocabulary: Types of Relationships

- **El amigo / La amiga** (Friend)
- **El novio / La novia** (Boyfriend / Girlfriend)
- **El esposo / La esposa** (Husband / Wife)
- **El compañero / La compañera** (Partner)
- **El vecino / La vecina** (Neighbor)

Descriptive Adjectives for Relationships

To describe the nature or quality of relationships, you might use:

- **Cercano/a** (Close)
- **Lejano/a** (Distant)
- **Amoroso/a** (Loving)
- **Complicado/a** (Complicated)
- **Supportivo/a** (Supportive)

Forming Sentences

Use the vocabulary to form sentences about your family and relationships, or to ask others about theirs. Remember to make adjectives agree in gender and number with the nouns they describe.

- **Mi madre es amorosa y supportiva.** (My mother is loving and supportive.)
- **Tengo dos hermanos y una hermana.** (I have two brothers and one sister.)
- **¿Cuántos primos tienes?** (How many cousins do you have?)

Practice Exercise

1. Write a short paragraph introducing your family or describing a close relationship. Include details such as names, ages, and personal qualities.
2. Create a set of questions you would ask someone about their family and relationships, aiming to use the new vocabulary.

Cultural Insight

Family plays a central role in many Spanish-speaking societies, often extending beyond the nuclear family to include a wide network of relatives. Discussions about family and relationships are common in social settings, reflecting the value placed on familial bonds and community. Understanding and respecting these cultural nuances when talking about family and relationships can deepen connections with Spanish speakers.

Congratulations on completing Day 41! You've expanded your ability to talk about one of the most universal and important aspects of human experience: family and relationships. This vocabulary not only enriches your conversations but also opens a window into the personal lives and cultural values of those you communicate with in Spanish. Tomorrow, we will explore vocabulary related to work and professional life, further broadening your language skills in new contexts. ¡Hasta mañana!

Day 42: Work and Professional Life

Welcome to Day 42, where we'll explore the vocabulary surrounding work and professional life. Discussing your job, career aspirations, and daily work tasks in Spanish can enhance both social interactions and professional opportunities. Today, we'll cover essential terms and phrases related to the workplace, job titles, and professional activities, enabling you to confidently engage in conversations about your professional life and inquire about others'.

Key Vocabulary: The Workplace

- **El trabajo** (Work, job)
- **La oficina** (Office)
- **La empresa / La compañía** (Company)
- **El colegio / La escuela** (School)
- **La universidad** (University)
- **El hospital** (Hospital)
- **La fábrica** (Factory)
- **El salario / El sueldo** (Salary, wage)
- **La entrevista de trabajo** (Job interview)
- **El currículum vitae** (Resume)

Job Titles and Professions

- **El ingeniero / La ingeniera** (Engineer)
- **El médico / La médica** (Doctor)
- **El profesor / La profesora** (Teacher)
- **El abogado / La abogada** (Lawyer)
- **El contador / La contadora** (Accountant)
- **El gerente / La gerente** (Manager)
- **El empleado / La empleada** (Employee)
- **El jefe / La jefa** (Boss)

Phrases for Discussing Work

- **¿En qué trabajas?** (What do you do [for work]?)
- **Trabajo en...** (I work in...)
- **Soy...** (I am a/an...)
- **Busco trabajo como...** (I'm looking for a job as a/an...)
- **Me especializo en...** (I specialize in...)
- **Tengo experiencia en...** (I have experience in...)

Describing Your Work Routine

- **Mis responsabilidades incluyen...** (My responsibilities include...)
- **Manejo... / Estoy a cargo de...** (I handle... / I'm in charge of...)
- **Trabajo a tiempo completo/parcial.** (I work full-time/part-time.)

- **Trabajo desde casa.** (I work from home.)

Practice Exercise

1. Create a brief professional bio for yourself or a fictional character, incorporating the job titles, workplace vocabulary, and phrases discussed. Include where you work, what your job title is, and a few key responsibilities or projects.

2. Formulate questions you might ask someone about their job in a networking event or social gathering, aiming to use the new vocabulary.

Cultural Insight

In many Spanish-speaking countries, professional life is seen as an extension of personal identity, and discussing work is common in both social and family settings. However, attitudes towards work-life balance, hierarchy, and workplace formality can vary widely across different cultures. Showing interest in someone's professional life is often appreciated, but always strive for respectful and context-appropriate inquiries.

Congratulations on completing Day 42! You've now equipped yourself with the language necessary to navigate discussions about work and professional life in Spanish. This new vocabulary not only enables you to share more about your own career but also helps you connect with others over shared professional interests or experiences. Tomorrow, we'll delve into the topic of education and schooling, further expanding your conversational scope. ¡Hasta mañana!

Day 43: Education and Schooling

On Day 43, we turn our focus to education and schooling, a universal topic that often surfaces in conversations, from discussing one's academic background to exploring educational systems in Spanish-speaking countries. Whether you're sharing your own experiences or inquiring about someone's studies, today's lesson will equip you with the vocabulary and phrases needed to navigate these discussions effectively.

Key Vocabulary: Education and Schooling

- **La educación** (Education)
- **La escuela** (School)
- **El colegio** (High school, also used for private schools)
- **La universidad** (University)
- **El instituto** (Institute, often used for secondary education)
- **El estudiante / La estudiante** (Student)
- **El profesor / La profesora** (Teacher)
- **La asignatura / La materia** (Subject)
- **El grado** (Grade, as in level or year)
- **La licenciatura** (Bachelor's degree)
- **La maestría** (Master's degree)

- **El doctorado** (Doctorate, PhD)
- **La beca** (Scholarship)
- **El examen** (Exam)
- **Los deberes / La tarea** (Homework)

Phrases for Discussing Education

- **Estudié en...** (I studied at...)
- **Me gradué en...** (I graduated in...)
- **Estoy estudiando...** (I am studying...)
- **Mi especialización es en...** (My major/specialization is in...)
- **Tengo un título en...** (I have a degree in...)
- **Quiero hacer un posgrado en...** (I want to do a postgraduate degree in...)

Discussing Educational Experiences

Talk about your educational journey, favorite subjects, memorable projects, or impactful teachers. Here's how you might structure such discussions:

- **Mi profesor/a de... me inspiró a...** (My teacher of... inspired me to...)
- **Lo que más me gustó de mi carrera fue...** (What I liked most about my degree was...)

Practice Exercise

1. Describe your educational background or that of a fictional character, including where you studied, what you studied, and any degrees or certifications obtained.

2. Write a dialogue between two old friends who are catching up and discussing their educational paths and current learning pursuits.

Cultural Insight

Education is highly valued across Spanish-speaking cultures, with each country having its unique system and traditions. From the importance of passing entrance exams to the celebration of graduations (often marked by significant ceremonies like the "graduación" or "acto de grado"), education forms a critical part of personal identity and societal progress. Discussing education can reveal insights into a person's interests, values, and aspirations, fostering deeper connections.

Congratulations on completing Day 43! Armed with the vocabulary and phrases to discuss education and schooling, you're prepared to engage in conversations that not only share your academic journey but also explore the rich educational landscapes of Spanish-speaking countries. This knowledge enhances your ability to connect on a personal level with others, reflecting shared experiences and mutual respect for learning. Tomorrow, we'll explore health, wellness, and navigating medical situations in Spanish, further broadening your communicative abilities. ¡Hasta entonces!

Day 44: Health, Wellness, and Emergencies

Welcome to Day 44, where we'll delve into an essential topic: health, wellness, and handling emergencies. The ability to discuss health issues, express how you're feeling, and navigate medical situations is crucial, especially for travelers or those living in Spanish-speaking countries. Today's lesson will provide you with the vocabulary and phrases needed to talk about health, describe symptoms, seek medical help, and discuss wellness practices.

Key Vocabulary: Health and Body

- **La salud** (Health)
- **El bienestar** (Well-being)
- **El cuerpo** (Body)
- **La cabeza** (Head)
- **El estómago** (Stomach)
- **El dolor** (Pain)
- **La fiebre** (Fever)
- **La gripe** (Flu)
- **La tos** (Cough)
- **El resfriado** (Cold)
- **La farmacia** (Pharmacy)

- **El hospital** (Hospital)
- **El médico/la médica** (Doctor)
- **La enfermera** (Nurse)

Phrases for Discussing Health

- **Me siento mal/bien.** (I feel bad/well.)
- **Tengo dolor de cabeza/estómago.** (I have a headache/stomachache.)
- **¿Dónde está el hospital/la farmacia más cercana?** (Where is the nearest hospital/pharmacy?)
- **Necesito ver a un médico.** (I need to see a doctor.)
- **¿Tiene algo para el dolor/la fiebre?** (Do you have anything for pain/fever?)

Talking About Wellness

Discussing wellness and healthy living is increasingly common. Here are some phrases to talk about wellness practices:

- **Hago ejercicio regularmente.** (I exercise regularly.)
- **Como alimentos saludables.** (I eat healthy foods.)
- **Me aseguro de descansar lo suficiente.** (I make sure to get enough rest.)

Handling Emergencies

Knowing how to communicate in medical emergencies is vital. Here are some phrases that could be life-saving:

- **¡Ayuda!** (Help!)
- **Llame a una ambulancia, por favor.** (Call an ambulance, please.)
- **Es una emergencia.** (It's an emergency.)
- **Estoy teniendo una reacción alérgica.** (I am having an allergic reaction.)

Practice Exercise

1. Write a dialogue between a patient and a doctor. Include the patient describing their symptoms and the doctor giving advice or prescribing treatment.

2. Create a weekly wellness plan in Spanish, detailing exercise routines, dietary preferences, and any mindfulness or relaxation practices you include for well-being.

Cultural Insight

Attitudes towards health and wellness can vary significantly across Spanish-speaking countries, influenced by traditional practices, healthcare systems, and societal norms. In many communities, home remedies and natural treatments are popular for minor ailments. Discussing health openly, especially asking about remedies or sharing advice, is often seen as a sign of care and community.

Congratulations on completing Day 44! You're now equipped with the language tools to discuss health issues, express feelings of wellness or illness, and navigate medical situations more confidently. This knowledge not only prepares you for emergencies but also enables you to participate in conversations about health and wellness, reflecting a universal aspect of human experience.

Tomorrow, we'll explore leisure activities, hobbies, and entertainment, adding another layer to your conversational repertoire. ¡Hasta mañana!

Day 45: Leisure, Entertainment, and Sports

Welcome to Day 45, where we shift our focus to the lighter side of life: leisure, entertainment, and sports. These topics frequently come up in conversations, offering a great way to connect with others through shared interests and activities. Today, you'll learn vocabulary and phrases that will help you talk about your hobbies, discuss movies or books, and chat about sports, whether you're a spectator or an active participant.

Vocabulary: Leisure and Entertainment

- **El ocio** (Leisure)

- **El pasatiempo** (Hobby)

- **La afición** (Hobby, interest)

- **La película** (Movie)

- **La serie** (TV series)

- **El concierto** (Concert)

- **La música** (Music)

- **El libro** (Book)

- **El juego** (Game)

- **El baile** (Dance)

- **El teatro** (Theater)

Vocabulary: Sports

- **El deporte** (Sport)
- **El partido** (Game, match)
- **El jugador/la jugadora** (Player)
- **El equipo** (Team)
- **Jugar** (to play) - Note that "jugar" changes to "juego" in the first person singular.
- **Entrenar** (to train)
- **Ganar** (to win)
- **Perder** (to lose)

Talking About Leisure Activities

To express your preferences or ask about someone else's, you might use:

- **Me gusta + [infinitive]/[noun].** (I like to...)
- **¿Qué te gusta hacer en tu tiempo libre?** (What do you like to do in your free time?)
- **Mi pasatiempo favorito es...** (My favorite hobby is...)

Discussing Entertainment

When talking about movies, music, or books, these phrases can be useful:

- **¿Has visto la última película de...?** (Have you seen the latest movie from...?)

- **Me encanta la música de...** (I love the music of...)
- **Estoy leyendo un libro sobre...** (I am reading a book about...)

Chatting About Sports

Whether you're discussing recent matches or favorite teams, here are some phrases to use:

- **¿Practicas algún deporte?** (Do you play any sports?)
- **Mi equipo favorito es...** (My favorite team is...)
- **Voy al gimnasio a entrenar.** (I go to the gym to train.)

Practice Exercise

1. Write about how you typically spend your weekends or leisure time, incorporating activities, sports, or entertainment preferences.
2. Create a dialogue between two friends making plans to attend a concert, including questions about musical preferences and logistical planning.

Cultural Insight

Leisure activities, entertainment, and sports play significant roles in Spanish-speaking societies, often reflecting broader cultural values and social dynamics. Festivals, football matches, and family gatherings centered around specific activities are common and highly valued. Sharing your interests and participating in discussions about local events can be a wonderful way to immerse yourself in the culture and connect with others on a personal level.

Congratulations on completing Day 45! You've now expanded your ability to engage in conversations about leisure, entertainment, and sports, enriching your interactions and allowing you to share more about your personal interests. These topics not only add enjoyment to our lives but also foster connections and understanding across cultures. Tomorrow, we'll delve into discussing work and professional life, further broadening your conversational scope. ¡Hasta entonces!

Days 46-50: Vocabulary Expansion Review

As we approach the conclusion of Part 5, the next five days are dedicated to reviewing, reinforcing, and expanding upon the vocabulary related to family and relationships, work and professional life, education and schooling, health and wellness, and leisure, entertainment, and sports. This period is crucial for solidifying your newfound knowledge, correcting any areas of misunderstanding, and integrating these vocabulary themes into your active language use.

Day 46: Family and Relationships Review

- **Exercise:** Create a family tree and label each member in Spanish, including their relationship to you. Describe each family member or friend with at least two adjectives (e.g., **Mi hermana es inteligente y divertida**).

- **Discussion:** Share stories or anecdotes about your family or close relationships with a language partner, focusing on using the vocabulary from Day 41.

Day 47: Work and Professional Life Review

- **Exercise:** Write a job advertisement in Spanish for your current position or dream job. Include job responsibilities, required qualifications, and workplace benefits.

- **Role-play:** Practice a job interview in Spanish with a partner, alternating roles between interviewer and candidate, utilizing the vocabulary from Day 42.

Day 48: Education and Schooling Review

- **Exercise:** Draft a personal statement in Spanish that you might use for a university application. Include your academic interests, achievements, and reasons for choosing your field of study.

- **Group Activity:** In a study group, discuss the education systems in your countries versus those in various Spanish-speaking countries, using the vocabulary from Day 43.

Day 49: Health, Wellness, and Emergencies Review

- **Exercise:** Simulate a doctor's visit in Spanish, where you describe symptoms of a common illness and the doctor (a language partner) advises treatment. Incorporate vocabulary from Day 44.

- **Reflection:** Write a brief essay on the importance of health and wellness, including activities you do to stay healthy, using as many terms from the health and wellness vocabulary as possible.

Day 50: Leisure, Entertainment, and Sports Review

- **Exercise:** Plan your ideal vacation or leisure day in Spanish, describing activities, entertainment options, and any sports you would include. Use the vocabulary from Day 45.

- **Creative Project:** Create a guide to your favorite hobby or sport in Spanish, explaining why you enjoy it, necessary equipment, and basic rules or techniques.

Additional Tips for Days 46-50:

- **Integrate Vocabulary in Daily Use:** Try to use the review topics in your daily conversations, whether it's talking about a movie you saw, a game you watched, or discussing your health and fitness routines.

- **Use Flashcards:** Create or update flashcards with the new vocabulary from this section. Regular review can significantly aid in retention.

- **Engage with Content:** Find articles, videos, podcasts, or books related to the five topics in Spanish. This will not only improve your vocabulary but also enhance listening and reading comprehension.

- **Language Exchange:** Utilize language exchange sessions to practice the vocabulary themes. Discussing a variety of topics can make these sessions more engaging and beneficial for both participants.

Congratulations on completing the Vocabulary Expansion Review of Part 5! You've done remarkable work deepening your understanding and use of Spanish vocabulary across a wide range of essential and interesting topics. This foundation will greatly enrich your conversations, allowing you to express yourself more fully and connect with others on a multitude of subjects. Continue practicing, exploring, and enjoying the journey of language learning. ¡Adelante y buena suerte!

Part 6: Days 51-60 - Mexican Culture and Slang

Day 51: Festivals and Holidays

Welcome to Day 51, where we dive into the vibrant world of Mexican festivals and holidays. Mexico's rich cultural tapestry is woven with traditions that celebrate its history, people, and religious beliefs. Understanding these celebrations provides insight into the heart and soul of Mexican life and allows for deeper connections and conversations when engaging with Mexican Spanish. Today, you'll learn about major festivals and holidays, along with vocabulary and expressions that will help you discuss these cultural events.

Major Mexican Festivals and Holidays

- **El Día de los Muertos** (Day of the Dead) - A celebration honoring deceased loved ones, marked by altars (ofrendas), colorful decorations, and traditional foods.

- **La Navidad** (Christmas) - Celebrated with family gatherings, posadas, and traditional foods leading up to Christmas Day.

- **La Semana Santa** (Holy Week) - Observing the last week of Lent with processions and religious ceremonies.

- **El Grito de Independencia** (Cry of Independence) - Mexico's Independence Day on September 16, celebrated with fireworks, parties, and the famous "grito" reenactment.

- **El Día de la Revolución** (Revolution Day) - Commemorating the start of the Mexican Revolution on November 20 with parades and civic ceremonies.

- **Las Fiestas de Octubre** (October Festivals) - A month-long celebration in Guadalajara featuring cultural events, concerts, and food.

Vocabulary for Discussing Festivals and Holidays

- **La fiesta** (Party/Festival)
- **El desfile** (Parade)
- **Los fuegos artificiales** (Fireworks)
- **La tradición** (Tradition)
- **El desfile** (Parade)
- **El baile** (Dance)
- **La música** (Music)
- **Los antojitos** (Traditional snacks or street food)

Expressions Related to Celebrations

- **¿Cómo celebras...?** (How do you celebrate...?)
- **Es una tradición familiar.** (It's a family tradition.)
- **Vamos a celebrar en grande.** (We're going to celebrate in a big way.)
- **Es mi fiesta favorita.** (It's my favorite holiday.)

Practice Exercise

1. Choose one Mexican festival or holiday and research how it's celebrated. Write a short paragraph describing the activities, foods, and traditions associated with this celebration.

2. Create a dialogue between two friends planning to attend one of these celebrations, including questions about what to expect, what to wear, and what traditions they might participate in.

Cultural Insight

Mexican festivals and holidays often blend indigenous traditions with Spanish colonial influences, creating unique celebrations known worldwide for their vibrancy, color, and depth. Participation in these festivities, even as a spectator, offers a profound way to experience Mexico's cultural richness firsthand. Understanding and respecting the significance behind these celebrations is crucial when engaging in discussions or festivities.

Congratulations on completing Day 51! You've just taken a significant step toward appreciating the cultural richness of Mexico through its festivals and holidays. This knowledge not only enriches your understanding of Mexican culture but also enhances your ability to connect on a deeper level with Spanish speakers during these celebratory times. Tomorrow, we'll explore Mexican food and culinary traditions, adding another layer to your cultural and linguistic journey. ¡Hasta mañana!

Day 52: Food and Culinary Traditions

Welcome to Day 52, where we indulge in the flavorsome world of Mexican food and culinary traditions. Mexican cuisine is a UNESCO Intangible Cultural Heritage of Humanity, celebrated for its diverse ingredients, complex flavors, and rich cultural significance. Today, we'll explore the vocabulary related to Mexican dishes, ingredients, and dining customs, allowing you to savor the language as much as the cuisine.

Key Vocabulary: Mexican Cuisine

- **La cocina mexicana** (Mexican cuisine)

- **El platillo** (Dish)

- **Los antojitos** (Street food snacks, literally "little cravings")

- **El maíz** (Corn)

- **Los frijoles** (Beans)

- **El chile** (Chili pepper)

- **La tortilla** (Tortilla)

- **El taco** (Taco)

- **La enchilada** (Enchilada)

- **El mole** (Mole, a traditional sauce)

- **El guacamole** (Guacamole)

- **La salsa** (Sauce)
- **El pozole** (Pozole, a traditional soup)
- **La tamales** (Tamales)

Phrases for Dining Out

When exploring Mexican cuisine, these phrases will enhance your dining experience:

- **¿Qué me recomienda?** (What do you recommend?)
- **Quisiera probar...** (I would like to try...)
- **¿Esto es picante?** (Is this spicy?)
- **Para llevar, por favor.** (To go, please.)
- **La cuenta, por favor.** (The bill, please.)

Discussing Food Preferences

Sharing your culinary preferences or dietary restrictions is crucial when dining with others or in restaurants:

- **Soy vegetariano/a.** (I am vegetarian.)
- **No puedo comer...** (I can't eat...)
- **Me encanta la comida mexicana.** (I love Mexican food.)
- **Prefiero sin picante.** (I prefer it not spicy.)

Practice Exercise

1. Write a short review in Spanish of your favorite Mexican dish, including descriptions of its flavors, ingredients, and why you enjoy it.

2. Create a dialogue between yourself and a street vendor where you're asking about their offerings, ordering food, and inquiring about specific ingredients or dietary accommodations.

Cultural Insight

Mexican cuisine is deeply tied to the country's history, geography, and cultural practices, with each region offering its unique dishes and flavors. Meals are often social occasions, bringing family and friends together to share in the tradition and joy of eating. Ingredients like corn, beans, and chili are staples, with ancient roots in Mexico's culinary history. Participating in Mexican culinary traditions, whether cooking at home or dining out, offers a delicious entry point into the culture.

Congratulations on completing Day 52! You've just added a flavorful dimension to your Spanish language skills, deepening your appreciation for Mexican cuisine and its cultural significance. Food is a universal language, and your ability to discuss Mexican culinary traditions will undoubtedly enrich your conversations and dining experiences. Tomorrow, we delve into music, dance, and art, further exploring the rich cultural expressions of Mexico. ¡Buen provecho y hasta mañana!

Day 53: Music, Dance, and Art

Welcome to Day 53, where we immerse ourselves in the vibrant world of Mexican music, dance, and art. These expressions of culture are fundamental to understanding the soul and spirit of Mexico, offering insights into the country's history, traditions, and contemporary life. Today, you'll learn about the diverse genres of Mexican music, traditional dances, and the rich tapestry of Mexican art, equipping you with the vocabulary to discuss these cultural manifestations.

Key Vocabulary: Music and Dance

- **La música** (Music)

- **La canción** (Song)

- **El baile** (Dance)

- **El mariachi** - A traditional Mexican music ensemble featuring violins, trumpets, and guitars.

- **La banda** - A brass-based form of traditional Mexican music.

- **El norteño** - A genre of Mexican music with German influences, featuring accordions and bajo sextos.

- **La cumbia** - A dance-oriented music genre with Colombian origins, popular in Mexico.

- **El folklórico** - Refers to traditional Mexican folk dance, characterized by colorful costumes and regional variations.

- **El ballet** - While globally understood, ballet in Mexico incorporates unique elements and often explores themes related to Mexican history and folklore.

Vocabulary: Art

- **El arte** (Art)
- **El mural** (Mural)
- **El pintor/la pintora** (Painter)
- **La escultura** (Sculpture)
- **El museo** (Museum)
- **La galería** (Gallery)
- **La exposición** (Exhibition)

Notable Figures:

- **Frida Kahlo** - Renowned for her self-portraits and works inspired by the nature and artifacts of Mexico.
- **Diego Rivera** - Famous for his large frescoes that helped establish the Mexican mural movement.
- **José Clemente Orozco** - A prolific muralist who focused on social and political critiques.

Phrases for Discussing Music, Dance, and Art

- **¿Quién es tu músico/pintor favorito?** (Who is your favorite musician/painter?)
- **Me encanta la música de...** (I love the music of...)

- **¿Has visto alguna vez el baile folklórico?** (Have you ever seen the folkloric dance?)
- **Quiero visitar el museo de...** (I want to visit the museum of...)

Practice Exercise

1. Choose a Mexican artist, musician, or dance genre you admire. Research and write a brief introduction in Spanish, including why they are significant within Mexican culture.
2. Create a dialogue between two friends planning to attend a Mexican music concert or art exhibition, discussing what they hope to see or experience.

Cultural Insight

Music, dance, and art are not just entertainment or aesthetic pursuits in Mexico; they are vital expressions of cultural identity, historical narrative, and social commentary. From the lively rhythms of mariachi and norteño to the profound visual narratives found in murals and paintings, these cultural forms invite engagement, reflection, and celebration. Participating in or observing these artistic expressions offers a deeper connection to the Mexican spirit and its global contributions.

Congratulations on completing Day 53! You've enriched your understanding of Mexican culture through its music, dance, and art. This knowledge not only enhances your cultural literacy but also provides a colorful backdrop for engaging in meaningful conversations about the artistic expressions that shape Mexico's identity. Tomorrow, we'll explore regional differences and dialects within Mexico, further expanding your cultural and linguistic horizons. ¡Hasta mañana!

Day 54: Regional Differences and Dialects

Welcome to Day 54, where we delve into the fascinating landscape of regional differences and dialects within Mexico. Mexico's vast geography and rich history have given rise to a diverse tapestry of linguistic expressions, accents, and vocabularies unique to various regions. Understanding these differences not only enriches your Spanish language skills but also deepens your appreciation of the cultural nuances that define Mexico's identity. Today, we'll explore some key regional distinctions and introduce you to vocabulary and phrases characteristic of different Mexican locales.

Regional Dialects in Mexico

- **Norteño** (Northern) - Characterized by a direct and straightforward style of speech, the northern dialect reflects the influence of ranch culture and its proximity to the United States.

- **Jalisquillo** (From Jalisco) - Known for the use of "cantadito," a sing-song intonation, particularly in areas like Guadalajara.

- **Chilango** (From Mexico City) - Distinctive for its urban slang and the influence of various internal migrations, making it one of the most dynamic dialects in Mexico.

- **Yucateco** (From Yucatán) - Influenced by Mayan languages, this dialect features unique words and expressions not found in other parts of Mexico.

Key Vocabulary and Expressions by Region

While standard Spanish is understood across Mexico, regional slang can vary significantly. Here are a few examples:

- **Güey** (Dude, guy) - Common in many parts of Mexico, especially in urban areas.

- **Chido** (Cool) - Widely used in central Mexico to describe something as cool or awesome.

- **Carnal** (Brother, close friend) - Used in the north and central regions.

- **Paro** (Favor) - "¿Me haces un paro?" is often heard in Mexico City, asking someone for a favor.

- **Aguas** (Watch out) - Used as a warning, akin to saying "Be careful!"

Practice Exercise

1. Choose two Mexican regions and research their unique dialects or linguistic features. Write a brief summary of each, including specific vocabulary, expressions, or pronunciations that distinguish them.

2. Create dialogues that showcase the regional slang or expressions you've learned. For example, a conversation between someone from Mexico City and someone from Monterrey, highlighting the differences in their speech.

Cultural Insight

Mexico's regional dialects are a testament to the country's rich cultural and historical diversity. These dialects do more than just mark geographic distinctions; they carry the stories, traditions, and identities of their people. Engaging with these regional variations fosters a deeper connection to Mexico's cultural heritage and enhances mutual understanding among its people. When traveling or interacting with individuals from different Mexican regions, showing interest in and respect for their local dialects and expressions can greatly enrich your experiences and relationships.

Congratulations on completing Day 54! Today's exploration into regional differences and dialects in Mexico has opened up a new dimension of the Spanish language, showcasing the beauty and diversity of Mexican Spanish. This knowledge not only prepares you for a richer linguistic experience but also equips you with a greater appreciation for the cultural nuances that define each region of Mexico. Tomorrow, we'll dive into Mexican slang and everyday expressions, adding even more color and authenticity to your Spanish conversations. ¡Hasta mañana!

Day 55: Slang and Everyday Expressions

Welcome to Day 55, where we dive into the lively world of Mexican slang and everyday expressions. Slang is the seasoning that gives language its flavor, and Mexican Spanish is particularly rich in colloquialisms. These expressions can vary widely across regions but are essential for anyone looking to speak Spanish in a way that feels natural and authentic. Today, we'll introduce you to some common Mexican slang and phrases that are popular across the country.

Understanding Mexican Slang

Mexican slang is deeply rooted in the country's culture and history, often reflecting social attitudes, humor, and creativity. While learning slang, it's important to understand the context in which these expressions are used, as some may be informal or inappropriate in certain situations.

Common Mexican Slang Terms

- **Padre** (Cool) - Used to describe something that is cool or awesome. "Esa película está muy padre."

- **Chamba** (Job/Work) - Refers to work or a job. "Estoy buscando chamba."

- **Güey** (Dude/Guy) - A very common term for referring to a person, similar to "dude" or "guy." Can be spelled as "wey" in informal contexts. "¿Qué onda, güey?"

- **Mande** (What?/Pardon?) - A polite way of asking someone to repeat themselves or saying "pardon?" "¿Mande? No entendí."

- **Aguas** (Watch out) - Used to warn someone to be careful. "¡Aguas con ese escalón!"

- **No manches** (No way/You're kidding) - Expression of disbelief or surprise. "No manches, ¿en serio ganaste?"

- **Cuate** (Friend) - Another word for a friend or buddy. "El cuate de allá es mi hermano."

- **Órale** (Wow/Okay/Let's go) - A versatile expression that can show surprise, agreement, or encouragement to take action. "Órale, está bien."

- **Chido** (Cool) - Another term for cool or great. "Ese concierto estuvo chido."

Everyday Expressions

- **¿Qué onda?** (What's up?) - A casual greeting among friends.

- **Sale y vale** (Okay, fine) - An expression of agreement or acknowledgment.

- **Ahorita** (Now/Later) - Interestingly, "ahorita" can mean right now or a little later, depending on the context.

Practice Exercise

1. Create a short dialogue incorporating as many of the slang terms and expressions introduced today. Imagine a conversation between friends making weekend plans.

2. Reflect on the use of slang in your native language or other languages you know. Write a short comparison of how slang functions in those languages versus Mexican Spanish.

Cultural Insight

Slang is a window into the collective psyche of a culture, offering insights into values, humor, and societal norms. In Mexico, the use of slang conveys warmth, familiarity, and a sense of belonging. However, because slang can be informal or even vulgar in certain contexts, it's crucial to understand when and with whom it's appropriate to use these expressions. Observing their use in real-life conversations, movies, or TV shows can provide valuable context.

Congratulations on completing Day 55! You've now added a layer of authenticity to your Spanish by familiarizing yourself with common Mexican slang and everyday expressions. This will not only make your conversations more natural but also help you understand and engage more deeply with Mexican culture. Tomorrow, we'll delve into professional and technical Spanish, broadening your ability to communicate in more formal or specialized contexts. ¡Hasta mañana!

DAYS 56-60: CULTURAL IMMERSION REVIEW

In the final stretch of Part 6, we dedicate these days to reviewing and immersing ourselves further into Mexican culture and slang, solidifying the vibrant linguistic and cultural knowledge we've acquired. This period is a chance to reflect on the rich tapestry of Mexican festivals, culinary traditions, music, art, regional dialects, and everyday expressions that bring language to life. Let's reinforce our learning and prepare to use our skills in real-world contexts.

Day 56: Review of Festivals and Holidays

- **Exercise:** Choose a Mexican festival or holiday you find fascinating and create a presentation or poster about it. Include its history, how it's celebrated, and any unique traditions or foods associated with it.

- **Cultural Exchange:** Share your presentation with a language exchange partner or in a study group. Discuss the similarities and differences between this festival and holidays in your own culture.

Day 57: Culinary Traditions Deep Dive

- **Exercise:** Cook a traditional Mexican dish or visit a Mexican restaurant. Document the experience, noting the ingredients, preparation steps, or cultural significance of the dish.

- **Discussion:** Write a review of the dish you prepared or tasted, describing its flavors, textures, and how it reflects Mexican culinary culture. Share this review in a language learning forum or with classmates.

Day 58: Music, Dance, and Art Appreciation

- **Exercise:** Explore a genre of Mexican music, a traditional dance, or the work of a Mexican artist. Create a playlist, learn a dance routine, or reproduce an art piece.

- **Reflection:** Reflect on how this artistic expression contributes to your understanding of Mexican culture. Discuss your thoughts in a journal entry or blog post.

Day 59: Regional Dialects and Slang Practice

- **Exercise:** Write a short story or dialogue that incorporates regional slang from two different areas of Mexico, highlighting the contrasts in language use.

- **Language Challenge:** Try to use at least five new slang expressions in conversations with Spanish speakers or in writing. Note the reactions and any new expressions you learn in return.

Day 60: Cultural Immersion Completion Project

- **Project:** Combine what you've learned into a comprehensive cultural project. This could be a video diary of your learning journey, a series of blog posts, a short documentary, or a creative piece that showcases the festivals, food, music, art, and slang you've explored.

- **Presentation:** Present your project to peers, teachers, or on a social media platform dedicated to language learning. Reflect on your growth in understanding Mexican culture and how this immersion has impacted your language skills.

Additional Tips for Days 56-60:

- **Active Engagement:** Seek out opportunities for live interaction with Mexican culture, whether through community events, music festivals, art exhibitions, or culinary experiences.

- **Media Immersion:** Watch Mexican films, listen to podcasts, or read books that highlight the cultural elements you've studied. This will enhance your comprehension and appreciation of the nuances within each context.

- **Language Practice:** Continue to practice speaking, writing, and thinking in Spanish, incorporating the cultural and slang terms you've learned. The more you use these expressions, the more naturally they'll come to you in conversation.

Congratulations on completing the Cultural Immersion Review of Part 6! You've taken significant steps toward not only learning the Spanish language but also embracing and understanding the richness of Mexican culture. This journey enhances your ability to communicate authentically and connect deeply with Spanish speakers, celebrating the diversity and vibrancy of their traditions and ways of life. Continue to explore, learn, and immerse yourself in new cultural experiences. ¡Felicidades y buena suerte en tu camino!

Part 7: Days 61-70 - Advanced Conversational Skills

Day 61: Advanced Dialogue Construction

Welcome to Day 61, where we elevate our conversational skills through advanced dialogue construction. Crafting dialogues that reflect nuanced thought, emotion, and cultural awareness is essential for engaging in meaningful conversations. Today, we'll focus on techniques for building complex dialogues, incorporating elements like conditional sentences, subjunctive mood, and idiomatic expressions to add depth and realism to your Spanish conversations.

Understanding Dialogue Structure

- **Opening:** Start with a greeting or a question that sets the tone for the conversation.

- **Body:** Develop the main topic through questions, answers, and shared information. Incorporate varied sentence structures and tenses to convey detailed information and express opinions.

- **Conclusion:** End with a summary of the discussion, a plan for future action, or an expression of gratitude.

Incorporating Complex Sentence Structures

- **Conditional Sentences:** Use these to discuss hypothetical situations. E.g., "Si tuviera más tiempo, aprendería a bailar salsa."

- **Subjunctive Mood:** Essential for expressing wishes, doubts, and emotions. E.g., "Es importante que todos participen en la conversación."

Using Idiomatic Expressions

Idioms add color and authenticity to your dialogues, reflecting real-life speech patterns. E.g., "Echarle ganas" (to put effort into something).

Practice Exercise

1. **Dialogue Writing:** Craft a dialogue between two characters planning a trip to a Mexican festival. Include:

- Their initial excitement and decision to go.

- A discussion of what they need to prepare or expect, using conditional sentences.

- Expressions of hopes or concerns about the trip, using the subjunctive mood.

- At least three idiomatic expressions relevant to travel or celebrations.

2. **Role-play:** With a partner, practice the dialogue. Pay attention to intonation, emotion, and the natural flow of conversation.

Tips for Advanced Dialogue Construction

- **Vary Your Vocabulary:** Avoid repetition by using synonyms and related terms.

- **Reflect Emotion:** Use adjectives, adverbs, and exclamation points to convey emotions effectively.

- **Cultural References:** Include references to cultural practices, cuisine, or landmarks to add depth to your dialogues.

- **Listen and Adapt:** Pay attention to how native speakers structure their dialogues, adopting phrases and patterns you observe.

Cultural Insight

Advanced dialogue skills not only improve your ability to communicate but also deepen your cultural understanding and sensitivity. Engaging with native speakers and consuming media in Spanish are invaluable for appreciating the subtleties of conversation that resonate with Spanish-speaking cultures.

Congratulations on completing Day 61! Today's focus on advanced dialogue construction equips you with the tools to create rich, engaging conversations that reflect a sophisticated grasp of Spanish. As you practice these skills, you'll find your ability to express complex ideas and emotions in Spanish growing, enhancing your interactions and relationships with Spanish speakers. Tomorrow, we'll explore strategies for maintaining a conversation, ensuring you can keep dialogues flowing smoothly and engagingly. ¡Hasta mañana!

Day 62: Subjunctive Mood and Expressing Doubt or Desire

Welcome to Day 62, where we delve deeper into the subjunctive mood, a crucial aspect of Spanish that allows you to express doubt, desire, emotion, uncertainty, and subjectivity. Mastering the subjunctive can add a layer of sophistication to your conversations, enabling you to articulate feelings and thoughts with greater nuance.

Understanding the Subjunctive Mood

The subjunctive mood is used in dependent clauses following specific expressions that imply doubt, desire, or emotion. Unlike the indicative mood, which states facts, the subjunctive conveys what the speaker feels about the action or wishes to happen.

Key Triggers for the Subjunctive

- **Expressions of Will and Influence:** *querer que* (to want that), *preferir que* (to prefer that), *sugerir que* (to suggest that).

- **Expressions of Emotion:** *alegrarse de que* (to be glad that), *sentir que* (to be sorry that), *temer que* (to fear that).

- **Expressions of Doubt or Denial:** *dudar que* (to doubt that), *no pensar que* (to not think that), *no creer que* (to not believe that).

- **Impersonal Expressions:** *es importante que* (it's important that), *es posible que* (it's possible that), *es necesario que* (it's necessary that).

Forming the Present Subjunctive

To form the present subjunctive:

1. Start with the "yo" form of the present indicative.

2. Drop the "-o" ending.

3. Add the opposite vowel endings: -ar verbs take "-e" endings, and -er/-ir verbs take "-a" endings.

- *Hablar -> hable, hables, hable, hablemos, habléis, hablen*

- *Comer -> coma, comas, coma, comamos, comáis, coman*

- *Vivir -> viva, vivas, viva, vivamos, viváis, vivan*

Practice Exercise

1. Write sentences expressing desires or emotions about future events using the subjunctive mood. For example, "Espero que tengamos buen tiempo mañana."

2. Create a dialogue between two friends, one expressing doubts about a decision and the other offering advice, using the subjunctive to reflect uncertainty and suggestions.

Advanced Usage: Past Subjunctive

For expressing doubt, desire, or emotion about past actions, the past subjunctive is used. It's formed by starting with the third person plural of the preterite tense, dropping the "-ron," and adding the past subjunctive endings (-ra, -ras, -ra, -ramos, -rais, -ran).

Cultural Insight

In Spanish-speaking cultures, expressing emotions, desires, and doubts is often more indirect than in English-speaking contexts. The subjunctive mood is a key tool for navigating these social nuances, allowing speakers to convey their feelings and thoughts in a way that respects the listener's perspective and leaves room for ambiguity.

Congratulations on completing Day 62! Today's exploration of the subjunctive mood has unlocked new ways for you to express complex emotions and thoughts in Spanish, enriching your conversations and deepening your connections. As you continue to practice, you'll find the subjunctive becoming a natural part of your expressive toolkit. Tomorrow, we'll focus on argumentation and debate skills, further enhancing your advanced conversational capabilities. ¡Hasta mañana!

Day 63: Narrating Stories and Past Events

On Day 63, we're focusing on the art of storytelling in Spanish, a vital skill for sharing experiences, recounting historical events, and engaging your audience in meaningful ways. Narrating in the past requires a good grasp of the various past tenses in Spanish and knowing when to use them to create a coherent and captivating story.

Key Past Tenses for Narration

- **Preterite (Pretérito):** Used for actions that were completed in the past, marking the beginning or end of an action. E.g., *Caminé por el parque ayer* (I walked through the park yesterday).

- **Imperfect (Imperfecto):** Describes ongoing past actions or states, setting the scene or describing habits. E.g., *Caminaba por el parque cuando...* (I was walking through the park when...).

- **Past Perfect (Pluscuamperfecto):** Indicates an action that had occurred before another action in the past. E.g., *Había caminado por el parque antes de llover* (I had walked through the park before it rained).

Structuring Your Story

1. **Setting the Scene:** Use the imperfect tense to describe the ongoing state or background of your story.

2. **Key Events:** Switch to the preterite to detail the specific actions that moved your story forward.

3. **Reflecting on Prior Events:** Employ the past perfect for actions that happened before the main events of your story.

Connecting Ideas

To make your story flow, use conjunctions and phrases that indicate time or sequence, such as *entonces* (then), *después* (afterwards), *antes de* (before), *mientras* (while), and *hasta que* (until).

Practice Exercise

1. Write a short story or personal anecdote about a memorable experience. Use the imperfect to set the scene, the preterite for the main actions, and the past perfect for any necessary background information.

2. With a partner, take turns sharing your stories. Listen for the use of past tenses and provide feedback on the clarity and flow of the narrative.

Cultural Insight

Storytelling is an essential part of Spanish-speaking cultures, often featuring vivid descriptions, emotional depth, and moral lessons. Stories are not just entertainment; they're a way to preserve history, impart values, and foster community connections. Understanding the cultural context behind stories can deepen your appreciation and enhance your storytelling skills.

Congratulations on completing Day 63! Mastering the art of narrating in Spanish enriches your conversations and allows you to share and connect through stories. Practice recounting your experiences and engaging with Spanish-language narratives to further hone your skills. Tomorrow, we'll explore expressing opinions and making arguments, key components of dynamic and thoughtful conversations. ¡Hasta mañana!

Day 64: Discussing Future Plans and Hypotheticals

Welcome to Day 64, where we'll focus on articulating future plans and exploring hypothetical scenarios in Spanish. These conversational skills are essential for discussing aspirations, making predictions, and engaging in speculative discussions—all of which add richness and depth to your interactions. Today, we'll delve into the future tense and the conditional mood, providing the tools you need to navigate conversations about what lies ahead or what could be.

The Future Tense

The future tense in Spanish is used not only to talk about upcoming events but also to express probability or conjecture about the present.

- **Formation:** For regular verbs, the future tense is formed by adding the endings *-é, -ás, -á, -emos, -éis, -án* directly to the infinitive, regardless of whether the verb ends in -ar, -er, or -ir.
  - E.g., *Hablar* becomes *hablaré, hablarás, hablará, hablaremos, hablaréis, hablarán*.
- **Usage:** To discuss planned activities, make predictions, and express likelihood.
  - E.g., *Mañana lloverá.* (It will rain tomorrow.)
  - E.g., *¿Dónde estará María?* (I wonder where María is?)

The Conditional Mood

The conditional mood is used to express what you would do in a hypothetical situation and is also employed for polite requests.

- **Formation:** Like the future tense, the conditional mood is formed by adding the endings *-ía, ías, ía, íamos, íais, ían* to the infinitive.
  - E.g., *Hablar* becomes *hablaría, hablarías, hablaría, hablaríamos, hablaríais, hablarían.*
- **Usage:** To discuss hypothetical situations and make polite requests.
  - E.g., *Si tuviera dinero, viajaría por el mundo.* (If I had money, I would travel the world.)
  - E.g., *¿Podrías pasarme la sal?* (Could you pass me the salt?)

Practice Exercise

1. **Future Plans:** Write a paragraph about your future plans for the next year, using the future tense. Include personal goals, travel plans, or any changes you anticipate.
2. **Hypothetical Situations:** Create a hypothetical situation (e.g., winning the lottery) and discuss what you would do in that scenario, using the conditional mood.

Advanced: Mixing Future and Conditional

For deeper conversations, practice using both tenses together to discuss how future plans might change under different conditions.

- E.g., *Si llueve mañana, cancelaré mi viaje.* (If it rains tomorrow, I will cancel my trip.)

Cultural Insight

In many Spanish-speaking cultures, discussing future plans and dreams is often intertwined with expressions of hope and ambition, reflecting a positive outlook on life. The conditional mood is frequently used to offer suggestions or advice, showing consideration for others' feelings and perspectives.

Congratulations on completing Day 64! You've gained valuable tools for discussing the future and hypothetical situations, enriching your ability to share aspirations and ponder life's possibilities in Spanish. These skills not only enhance your conversational range but also allow for deeper connections through shared dreams and speculative thinking. Tomorrow, we'll explore strategies for effective argumentation and debate in Spanish, further refining your advanced conversational skills. ¡Hasta mañana!

Day 65: Persuading and Negotiating

On Day 65, we delve into the nuanced skills of persuasion and negotiation in Spanish. Whether you're discussing plans with friends, debating viewpoints, or navigating professional negotiations, the ability to persuade and negotiate is invaluable. This lesson will focus on strategic language use for making compelling arguments, expressing preferences clearly, and reaching mutual agreements.

Key Vocabulary for Persuasion and Negotiation

- **Convencer** (to convince)

- **Persuadir** (to persuade)

- **Negociar** (to negotiate)

- **La propuesta** (proposal)

- **El acuerdo** (agreement)

- **El compromiso** (commitment)

- **La concesión** (concession)

- **El conflicto** (conflict)

- **Los términos** (terms)

- **Los beneficios** (benefits)

Expressions for Persuasion

- **Te recomiendo que...** (I recommend that you...)
- **Sería mejor si...** (It would be better if...)
- **¿Has considerado...?** (Have you considered...?)
- **Desde mi punto de vista...** (From my point of view...)
- **No te olvides de...** (Don't forget about...)

Techniques for Negotiation

- **Escuchar activamente** (Active listening) - Show that you understand the other person's perspective before presenting your own.
- **Buscar un terreno común** (Finding common ground) - Highlight agreements to build a foundation for consensus.
- **Hacer preguntas abiertas** (Asking open-ended questions) - Encourage dialogue and clarify positions.
- **Proponer soluciones alternativas** (Proposing alternative solutions) - Offer options to move the negotiation forward.

Practice Exercise

1. **Persuasion Scenario:** Write a dialogue where you try to persuade a friend to join you on a trip to Mexico, using at least three of the expressions for persuasion. Include potential objections they might have and how you would respond.

2. **Negotiation Role-play:** With a partner, role-play a negotiation scenario, such as deciding on a project plan or resolving a scheduling conflict. Practice using the negotiation techniques and aim for a mutually satisfactory agreement.

Advanced: The Subjunctive in Persuasion

The subjunctive mood often appears in persuasive speech to express desires, doubts, and hypothetical situations.

- **Es importante que lo consideres.** (It's important that you consider it.)
- **Quiero que sepas que...** (I want you to know that...)

Cultural Insight

In Spanish-speaking cultures, personal relationships often influence persuasion and negotiation. Building rapport and demonstrating respect are as important as the arguments themselves. Understanding cultural norms and values can significantly enhance your effectiveness in persuasion and negotiation within these contexts.

Congratulations on completing Day 65! You've equipped yourself with essential strategies for persuading and negotiating in Spanish, enhancing your ability to engage in complex interactions and discussions. These skills not only serve practical purposes in everyday situations but also foster deeper, more meaningful connections through respectful and constructive dialogue. Tomorrow, we'll continue to refine your conversational skills by exploring how to express emotions and reactions in Spanish. ¡Hasta mañana!

DAYS 66-70: ADVANCED COMMUNICATION REVIEW

In the final stretch of Part 7, we dedicate these days to consolidating and expanding upon the advanced communication skills you've developed. This period is your opportunity to refine your abilities in crafting nuanced dialogues, expressing complex ideas, and engaging in sophisticated conversations that span a range of topics from personal aspirations to cultural insights.

Day 66: Review of Advanced Dialogue Construction

- **Exercise:** Craft a comprehensive dialogue that incorporates various tenses, the subjunctive mood, and idiomatic expressions, based on a scenario involving a significant life decision. Focus on creating depth and realism in the conversation.

- **Feedback:** Share your dialogue with peers or a tutor and ask for feedback on flow, grammatic accuracy, and the naturalness of expression.

Day 67: Subjunctive Mood and Expressing Complex Ideas

- **Exercise:** Write a series of exchanges where the subjunctive mood is used to express hopes, doubts, and hypothetical scenarios. Include a variety of triggers such as expressions of emotion, impersonal expressions, and recommendations.

- **Challenge:** Engage in a conversation with a language exchange partner where you discuss future plans or make suggestions for a hypothetical project, using the subjunctive mood throughout.

Day 68: Narrating Stories and Reflecting on Past Experiences

- **Exercise:** Narrate a memorable personal experience or a historical event, using a mix of past tenses for accuracy and effect. Pay particular attention to setting the scene, describing actions, and reflecting on the outcomes or lessons learned.

- **Discussion:** Present your narrative to a study group or tutor and discuss the use of different past tenses. Explore how changing tenses impacts the story's clarity and emotional resonance.

Day 69: Discussing Future Plans and Hypotheticals

- **Exercise:** Develop a plan for an ideal future event, such as a dream vacation or career goal. Use the future tense to outline the plan and the conditional mood to discuss hypothetical aspects or alternatives.

- **Simulation:** Simulate a planning session with peers, where you negotiate roles, responsibilities, and contingencies for a collaborative project, using future and conditional tenses.

Day 70: Advanced Communication Completion Project

- **Project:** Combine the communication skills you've honed into a final project. This could be a video presentation, a written essay, or a creative narrative that showcases your ability to use advanced Spanish in meaningful conversation.

- **Presentation:** Share your project with your language learning community, providing insights into your learning journey, challenges overcome, and areas for future growth. Solicit feedback on your use of language and communication strategies.

Additional Tips for Days 66-70:

- **Reflective Practice:** After each exercise or conversation, take time to reflect on what went well and areas where you felt challenged. Identify specific goals for continued practice.

- **Diverse Media Consumption:** Immerse yourself in Spanish-language media that covers a wide range of topics and styles. Pay attention to the use of advanced grammatical structures and try to incorporate what you learn into your speaking and writing.

- **Continuous Engagement:** Keep seeking out opportunities for conversation, whether through language exchanges, discussion groups, or social media platforms. Real-world practice is key to mastering advanced communication skills.

Congratulations on completing the Advanced Communication Review of Part 7! You've made significant strides in enhancing your conversational abilities, preparing you for engaging discussions, and deep connections in Spanish. Continue to practice, explore, and immerse yourself in new linguistic and cultural experiences. Your journey to mastery is ongoing, and each conversation is a step forward. ¡Felicidades y adelante con tu aprendizaje!

Part 8: Days 71-80 - Practical Applications for Fluency

Day 71: Problem Solving in Spanish

Welcome to Day 71, where we focus on problem-solving in Spanish, a crucial skill for navigating challenges, misunderstandings, and conflicts in Spanish-speaking contexts. Whether you're dealing with a travel mishap, workplace issue, or personal misunderstanding, the ability to articulate problems and negotiate solutions in Spanish is invaluable. Today, we'll explore vocabulary, phrases, and strategies for effective problem-solving.

Vocabulary for Problem Solving

- **El problema** (Problem)
- **La solución** (Solution)
- **El desafío / El reto** (Challenge)
- **El conflicto** (Conflict)
- **La malentendido** (Misunderstanding)
- **Resolver** (To solve)
- **Negociar** (To negotiate)
- **La queja** (Complaint)
- **La explicación** (Explanation)
- **Acordar / Llegar a un acuerdo** (To agree / To reach an agreement)

Expressing a Problem

- **Tengo un problema con...** (I have a problem with...)
- **Me enfrento a un desafío relacionado con...** (I'm facing a challenge related to...)
- **Hay un conflicto entre... y...** (There's a conflict between... and...)

Proposing Solutions

- **Una posible solución sería...** (A possible solution would be...)
- **¿Qué te parece si...?** (How about if we...?)
- **Podríamos intentar...** (We could try...)

Negotiating and Reaching Agreements

- **Estoy dispuesto/a a... si tú...** (I'm willing to... if you...)
- **¿Podemos encontrar un punto medio?** (Can we find a middle ground?)
- **Vamos a comprometernos a...** (Let's commit to...)

Practice Exercise

1. **Problem Description:** Write a brief description of a problem you've encountered in a Spanish-speaking context or invent a scenario. Include what the problem is, whom it involves, and its potential impact.

2. **Solution Proposal:** Draft a dialogue between the parties involved, where you articulate the problem, propose solutions, and negotiate an agreement. Use the vocabulary and phrases introduced above.

Tips for Effective Problem Solving

- **Stay Calm and Objective:** Keep the conversation focused on resolving the issue rather than assigning blame.

- **Listen Actively:** Make sure to understand the other party's perspective fully before responding.

- **Be Open to Compromise:** Flexibility can lead to more effective and mutually satisfactory solutions.

Cultural Insight

In many Spanish-speaking cultures, direct confrontation is often avoided, and a more indirect approach to problem-solving may be preferred. Emphasizing harmony, saving face, and fostering positive relationships can be as important as resolving the issue itself. Understanding these cultural nuances can guide your problem-solving efforts and help maintain respectful and constructive interactions.

Congratulations on completing Day 71! You've equipped yourself with essential tools for problem-solving in Spanish, enhancing your ability to navigate challenges effectively while fostering understanding and cooperation. As you continue to apply these skills, you'll find that overcoming obstacles in Spanish-speaking environments becomes more manageable and rewarding. Tomorrow, we'll focus on expressing and handling emotions in Spanish, further expanding your communicative competence. ¡Hasta mañana!

Day 72: Making Complaints and Resolving Conflicts

On Day 72, we navigate the delicate process of making complaints and resolving conflicts in Spanish. Whether it's addressing a service issue, expressing dissatisfaction, or mediating disputes, handling such situations with tact and clarity is crucial. Today's lesson focuses on the language and strategies necessary for articulating complaints constructively and working towards resolution.

Vocabulary for Making Complaints

- **La queja** (Complaint)

- **Insatisfecho/a** (Dissatisfied)

- **El reembolso** (Refund)

- **La compensación** (Compensation)

- **El malentendido** (Misunderstanding)

- **El servicio al cliente** (Customer service)

- **El error** (Error, mistake)

- **La solución** (Solution)

Phrases for Expressing Dissatisfaction

- **Quiero hacer una queja sobre...** (I want to make a complaint about...)

- **No estoy satisfecho/a con...** (I'm not satisfied with...)
- **Ha habido un problema con...** (There has been a problem with...)
- **Es inaceptable que...** (It's unacceptable that...)

Strategies for Conflict Resolution

- **Expresar la situación claramente** (Express the situation clearly) - Be specific about what went wrong and how it affected you.
- **Escuchar la otra parte** (Listen to the other party) - Understanding their perspective can facilitate a smoother resolution.
- **Proponer una solución justa** (Propose a fair solution) - Suggest what would make the situation right for you, but be open to compromise.
- **Mantener la calma y ser respetuoso/a** (Stay calm and be respectful) - Even in frustration, respectful communication leads to better outcomes.

Practice Exercise

1. **Complaint Scenario:** Write a scenario where you have to lodge a complaint in Spanish—perhaps a faulty product, poor service at a restaurant, or an incorrect bill. Detail the issue and how it impacted you.

2. **Resolution Dialogue:** Create a dialogue between you and a representative (e.g., waiter, customer service agent) addressing the complaint. Use the phrases for expressing dissatisfaction and aim to reach a resolution by the end of the exchange.

Additional Phrases for Seeking Resolution

- **¿Cómo podemos solucionar este problema?** (How can we solve this problem?)

- **Me gustaría recibir un reembolso/una compensación.** (I would like to receive a refund/compensation.)

- **Gracias por su comprensión y ayuda.** (Thank you for your understanding and help.)

Cultural Insight

In many Spanish-speaking cultures, direct confrontation is often avoided, and a softer approach to complaints and conflict resolution is preferred. Emphasizing the collective desire for a solution and showing appreciation for the other party's assistance can facilitate a positive resolution. Understanding these cultural nuances is key to effective communication in conflict situations.

Congratulations on completing Day 72! Mastering the art of making complaints and resolving conflicts in Spanish equips you with valuable communication tools, ensuring you can navigate challenging situations with confidence and grace. Tomorrow, we'll explore how to share and discuss news and current events in Spanish, further broadening your conversational scope. ¡Hasta mañana!

Day 73: Planning Events and Hosting

Welcome to Day 73, where we focus on the language of planning events and hosting in Spanish. Organizing gatherings, from casual meet-ups to formal celebrations, requires clear communication and attention to detail. Today, we'll cover essential vocabulary and phrases to help you invite guests, discuss arrangements, and ensure your event runs smoothly, all while fostering a warm and welcoming atmosphere.

Vocabulary for Event Planning

- **El evento** (Event)
- **La fiesta** (Party)
- **La reunión** (Meeting/Gathering)
- **La celebración** (Celebration)
- **El invitado/la invitada** (Guest)
- **La invitación** (Invitation)
- **Confirmar** (To confirm)
- **Organizar** (To organize)
- **La decoración** (Decoration)
- **El menú** (Menu)
- **El lugar** (Place/Location)

- **La fecha** (Date)
- **La hora** (Time)

Phrases for Invitations and Arrangements

- **Te invito a...** (I invite you to...)
- **¿Te gustaría asistir a...?** (Would you like to attend...?)
- **¿Puedes confirmar tu asistencia?** (Can you confirm your attendance?)
- **La fiesta será en...** (The party will be at...)
- **¿Qué te parece si...?** (How about if we...?)

Discussing Details and Preferences

- **¿Tienes alguna preferencia alimentaria?** (Do you have any dietary preferences?)
- **Vamos a decorar el lugar con...** (We're going to decorate the place with...)
- **¿Cuál es el mejor horario para ti?** (What's the best time for you?)
- **Necesito tu ayuda para...** (I need your help with...)

Practice Exercise

1. **Event Invitation:** Write an invitation for an event you're planning. Include the type of event, date, time, location, and any special instructions or requests for guests.//
2. **Planning Dialogue:** Create a dialogue between you and a friend or vendor discussing preparations for the event. Focus on

arrangements such as the menu, decorations, or entertainment options.

Tips for Successful Hosting

- **Anticipate Needs:** Consider the comfort and preferences of your guests in every aspect of planning.

- **Be Flexible:** Be prepared to adapt as plans evolve or unexpected situations arise.

- **Express Appreciation:** Show gratitude to your guests for attending and any contributions they make.

Cultural Insight

Hospitality is a cherished value in Spanish-speaking cultures, often characterized by warmth, generosity, and a focus on communal enjoyment. Events and gatherings are seen as opportunities to strengthen bonds and create lasting memories. Emphasizing the communal aspect of your event and the joy of sharing experiences can resonate deeply with guests from these cultures.

Congratulations on completing Day 73! You're now better equipped to plan and host events in Spanish, enhancing your ability to bring people together and create meaningful, enjoyable gatherings. The skills you've developed are valuable for both personal and professional contexts, ensuring you can navigate event planning with confidence and cultural sensitivity. Tomorrow, we'll explore expressing and handling emotions in Spanish, a crucial aspect of personal communication. ¡Hasta entonces!

Day 74: Traveling and Adventure

Welcome to Day 74, where we embark on the exciting topics of traveling and adventure in Spanish. Discussing travel plans, sharing experiences from past trips, and dreaming about future destinations are fantastic ways to connect with others and practice your Spanish. Today, we'll cover essential vocabulary and expressions related to travel, making it easier for you to navigate these discussions and plan your adventures.

Vocabulary for Travel and Adventure

- **El viaje** (Trip)
- **Viajar** (To travel)
- **El destino** (Destination)
- **La reserva** (Reservation)
- **El alojamiento** (Accommodation)
- **El pasaje/el boleto** (Ticket)
- **El pasaporte** (Passport)
- **La maleta** (Suitcase)
- **El equipaje** (Luggage)
- **El vuelo** (Flight)
- **La aventura** (Adventure)

- **Explorar** (To explore)
- **La excursión** (Excursion, tour)
- **El itinerario** (Itinerary)

Expressions for Discussing Travel Plans

- **¿A dónde piensas viajar?** (Where do you plan to travel?)
- **Voy a hacer un viaje a...** (I'm going to take a trip to...)
- **¿Qué me recomiendas visitar en...?** (What do you recommend visiting in...?)
- **Estoy buscando recomendaciones para...** (I'm looking for recommendations for...)
- **Tengo planeado explorar...** (I plan to explore...)

Sharing Travel Experiences

- **Uno de mis viajes favoritos fue a...** (One of my favorite trips was to...)
- **Lo que más me gustó de... fue...** (What I liked the most about... was...)
- **Una aventura inolvidable que tuve fue...** (An unforgettable adventure I had was...)
- **Aprendí mucho sobre... durante mi viaje.** (I learned a lot about... during my trip.)

Practice Exercise

1. **Travel Itinerary:** Create an itinerary for a dream trip to a Spanish-speaking country. Include destinations, activities, and any cultural sites you'd like to visit.

2. **Travel Story:** Write a short narrative about a memorable travel experience you've had or would like to have. Focus on describing the places, the people, and any significant moments.

Planning and Adventure Tips

- **Be Open to New Experiences:** Travel often brings unexpected opportunities. Be open to exploring off the beaten path.

- **Learn Local Phrases:** Knowing local expressions and slang can enhance your travel experience and help you connect with locals.

- **Respect Cultural Norms:** Take time to understand and respect the customs and traditions of the places you visit.

Cultural Insight

Traveling in Spanish-speaking countries offers a rich tapestry of cultures, landscapes, and histories to explore. From the bustling streets of Buenos Aires to the stunning beaches of the Caribbean, each destination has its unique charm and challenges. Engaging with locals and experiencing the culture firsthand can provide invaluable insights and make your travel more rewarding.

Congratulations on completing Day 74! Armed with the language skills for discussing travel and adventures, you're well-prepared to share your experiences, dream up new journeys, and engage with fellow travelers and locals alike. Embrace the spirit of adventure, and let your language skills guide you to unforgettable experiences. Tomorrow, we'll delve into health and fitness, expanding your conversational range further. ¡Buen viaje!

Day 75: Technology and the Internet

Welcome to Day 75, where we explore the ever-evolving world of technology and the internet. As these areas become increasingly integral to daily life, being able to discuss tech trends, digital tools, and online experiences in Spanish is invaluable. Today, we'll dive into vocabulary and expressions that will help you navigate conversations about the digital world, from social media to cybersecurity.

Vocabulary for Technology and the Internet

- **La tecnología** (Technology)

- **El internet** (The internet)

- **La red social** (Social network)

- **El sitio web** (Website)

- **La aplicación (app)** (Application, app)

- **El correo electrónico** (Email)

- **La cuenta** (Account)

- **La contraseña** (Password)

- **El usuario** (User)

- **El dispositivo móvil** (Mobile device)

- **La tableta** (Tablet)

- **El ordenador/la computadora** (Computer)
- **La seguridad cibernética** (Cybersecurity)
- **La inteligencia artificial** (Artificial intelligence)

Expressions for Discussing Technology

- **¿Qué aplicaciones usas regularmente?** (What apps do you use regularly?)
- **Me mantengo conectado/a a través de...** (I stay connected through...)
- **Prefiero... a...** (I prefer... over...)
- **Estoy aprendiendo a usar...** (I'm learning to use...)
- **Sigo muchos blogs sobre...** (I follow many blogs about...)

Talking About Online Experiences

- **Comparto fotos en...** (I share photos on...)
- **Leo noticias en...** (I read news on...)
- **Compro en línea en...** (I shop online at...)
- **Me preocupa la privacidad en...** (I'm concerned about privacy on...)

Practice Exercise

1. **Tech Preferences Dialogue:** Write a dialogue between two friends discussing their favorite apps, websites, and technology gadgets. Include opinions and recommendations.

2. **Cybersecurity Tips:** Create a list of recommendations for maintaining online security and privacy in Spanish. Imagine you're advising someone who is new to using the internet.

Tips for Keeping Up with Tech in Spanish

- **Follow Spanish-Language Tech Blogs:** Stay informed about the latest tech trends by following blogs and news sites in Spanish.

- **Use Tech-Related Vocabulary Regularly:** Incorporate technology vocabulary into your daily conversations or journaling to reinforce learning.

- **Participate in Online Forums:** Engage in discussions on tech topics in Spanish-speaking forums to practice your language skills and gain new insights.

Cultural Insight

The rapid adoption of technology and the internet across Spanish-speaking countries has transformed communication, entertainment, and commerce. However, the digital divide remains a significant issue, with access to technology varying widely. Discussions about technology in Spanish often reflect broader conversations about progress, inequality, and the future.

Congratulations on completing Day 75! You're now better equipped to discuss the digital age in Spanish, from the latest app trends to concerns about online privacy. As technology continues to evolve, so too will the language we use to talk about it. Stay curious and continue expanding your tech vocabulary as you engage with the Spanish-speaking world. Tomorrow, we delve into environmental issues and sustainability, topics of global importance and interest. ¡Hasta mañana!

Days 76-80: Real-World Spanish Use Review

As we approach the culmination of Part 8, these final days are dedicated to reinforcing and applying the practical Spanish skills you've developed. Focused on real-world usage, this review period emphasizes integrating language into daily life, from navigating travel and technology to engaging in discussions about global issues. Let's refine your ability to use Spanish confidently in diverse contexts.

Day 76: Comprehensive Travel Dialogue Review

- **Exercise:** Reflect on your dream Spanish-speaking destination and outline a detailed plan, including travel, accommodation, sightseeing, and dining. Write a dialogue between yourself and a travel agent, local guide, or host, using vocabulary and expressions from the travel section.

- **Discussion:** Share your travel plan and dialogue with peers or a language exchange partner. Get feedback on realism, language use, and cultural appropriateness.

Day 77: Technology in Daily Life

- **Exercise:** Think about how technology impacts your daily routine. Write a journal entry or blog post in Spanish detailing your typical tech interactions, favorite apps, and online habits. Discuss any concerns you have about digital trends or cybersecurity.

- **Presentation:** Present your thoughts on technology and its role in society to a Spanish-speaking audience, either in a virtual meeting, language class, or video format. Encourage questions and comments to foster discussion.

Day 78: Environmental Awareness Conversation

- **Exercise:** Research an environmental issue affecting a Spanish-speaking country or the global community. Prepare a short presentation or argument in Spanish, proposing solutions or actions individuals and communities can take.

- **Debate:** Organize a debate or discussion group to talk about environmental challenges and sustainability. Use the information and perspectives gathered to engage in a meaningful exchange of ideas.

Day 79: Problem-Solving Scenarios Practice

- **Exercise:** Create complex problem-solving scenarios you might encounter, such as organizing a community event, resolving a dispute among friends, or addressing a customer service issue. Write out the scenario, your approach to solving the problem, and the dialogue involved.

- **Role-Play:** Act out these scenarios with a partner or group, practicing the negotiation, persuasion, and conflict-resolution skills you've learned. Reflect on the effectiveness of your communication strategies.

Day 80: Real-World Spanish Application Project

- **Project:** Combine the skills and knowledge from the previous days into a comprehensive project that showcases your ability to use Spanish in real-world contexts. This could be a video tour guide of a Spanish-speaking area, a podcast episode discussing a tech innovation, or an article on environmental activism in the Spanish-speaking world.

- **Reflection:** Share your project with your language learning community, teachers, or peers. Reflect on your growth in Spanish, areas for improvement, and goals for continued language acquisition.

Additional Tips for Days 76-80:

- **Immersive Learning:** Engage with Spanish media, podcasts, and literature that cover the topics you've explored. This immersion reinforces learning and exposes you to diverse perspectives.

- **Community Engagement:** Use social media, forums, and language exchange sites to discuss your interests and opinions in Spanish. Real-time interaction sharpens your communicative skills and builds confidence.

- **Continuous Practice:** Incorporate Spanish into your daily life as much as possible. From writing to-do lists to thinking through plans in Spanish, every bit of practice helps solidify your language skills.

Congratulations on completing the Real-World Spanish Use Review! Over the past days, you've honed your ability to navigate complex conversations, articulate ideas, and engage with pressing global issues in Spanish. This journey through practical applications for fluency underscores the power of language to connect us across cultures and communities. Continue to explore, learn, and communicate, letting your curiosity and passion for Spanish guide you to new horizons. ¡Felicidades y adelante con tus aventuras en español!

Part 9: Days 81-90 - Professional and Technical Spanish

Day 81: Business and Commerce Language

Welcome to Day 81, where we dive into the language of business and commerce in Spanish. Whether you're engaging in professional conversations, navigating the business world, or discussing economic trends, mastering this specialized vocabulary and set of expressions is crucial. Today, we'll cover essential terms and phrases that will help you communicate effectively in business settings and understand commerce-related discussions.

Key Vocabulary for Business and Commerce

- **El negocio** (Business)
- **La empresa** (Company)
- **El comercio** (Commerce)
- **El mercado** (Market)
- **La marca** (Brand)
- **El producto** (Product)
- **El servicio** (Service)
- **El cliente** (Client)
- **El consumidor** (Consumer)
- **La venta** (Sale)
- **La estrategia de marketing** (Marketing strategy)

- **El análisis de mercado** (Market analysis)
- **La competencia** (Competition)
- **El acuerdo comercial** (Trade agreement)
- **La reunión de negocios** (Business meeting)

Phrases for Business Conversations

- **¿Cuál es tu rol en la empresa?** (What is your role in the company?)
- **Estamos buscando expandir nuestro mercado.** (We are looking to expand our market.)
- **¿Podemos hablar sobre el acuerdo comercial?** (Can we talk about the trade agreement?)
- **Nuestra marca se distingue por...** (Our brand is distinguished by...)
- **¿Cuál es su estrategia de marketing?** (What is your marketing strategy?)

Discussing Business Plans and Strategies

- **Nuestro objetivo es...** (Our goal is...)
- **Estamos enfocados en...** (We are focused on...)
- **La clave para nuestro éxito es...** (The key to our success is...)
- **Estamos enfrentando desafíos con...** (We are facing challenges with...)

Practice Exercise

1. **Business Pitch:** Prepare a pitch for a hypothetical or real business product or service you are passionate about. Include information about the company, the target market, the unique selling proposition, and future goals.

2. **Business Meeting Simulation:** Write a dialogue simulating a business meeting where you discuss a potential partnership, product launch, or marketing strategy. Incorporate negotiation phrases and discuss terms and conditions.

Tips for Business Language Proficiency

- **Stay Informed:** Keep up-to-date with business news and trends in Spanish-speaking markets by following relevant news outlets and industry publications.

- **Practice Specific Vocabulary:** Regularly review and practice business-related vocabulary to enhance your fluency in professional settings.

- **Cultural Sensitivity:** Understand cultural nuances in business practices among different Spanish-speaking countries to communicate more effectively and respectfully.

Cultural Insight

Business practices and etiquette can vary significantly across Spanish-speaking countries. For example, personal relationships and trust are often considered as important as the business proposition itself. Being aware of these cultural nuances can greatly impact the success of your business interactions and negotiations.

Congratulations on completing Day 81! You've taken a significant step toward navigating the business and commerce landscape in Spanish. This foundational knowledge will not only enhance your professional communication but also open doors to new opportunities in the global market. Tomorrow, we'll explore the language of finance and banking, further expanding your professional Spanish skills. ¡Hasta mañana!

DAY 82: TECHNICAL TERMS FOR IT AND DIGITAL MEDIA

Welcome to Day 82, where we delve into the specialized language of Information Technology (IT) and digital media. As the digital landscape continues to evolve, proficiency in this technical vocabulary is essential for professionals working in tech fields, digital marketing, web development, and related areas. Today, we'll introduce key terms and expressions in Spanish that are fundamental for discussing IT and digital media topics.

Key Vocabulary for IT

- **La informática** (Information technology)
- **El software** (Software)
- **El hardware** (Hardware)
- **La base de datos** (Database)
- **La red** (Network)
- **El servidor** (Server)
- **La programación** (Programming)
- **El desarrollador / La desarrolladora** (Developer)
- **El diseño web** (Web design)
- **La seguridad informática** (Cybersecurity)
- **El almacenamiento en la nube** (Cloud storage)

- **La inteligencia artificial (IA)** (Artificial intelligence, AI)
- **El aprendizaje automático** (Machine learning)
- **La realidad virtual (RV)** (Virtual reality, VR)

Key Vocabulary for Digital Media

- **Los medios digitales** (Digital media)
- **La red social** (Social network)
- **El contenido** (Content)
- **La campaña digital** (Digital campaign)
- **El marketing digital** (Digital marketing)
- **El blog** (Blog)
- **El influencer** (Influencer)
- **La analítica web** (Web analytics)
- **El posicionamiento en buscadores (SEO)** (Search engine optimization, SEO)
- **La publicidad en línea** (Online advertising)

Phrases for Discussing IT and Digital Media

- **Estamos desarrollando un nuevo software para...** (We are developing new software for...)
- **¿Podrías actualizar la base de datos?** (Could you update the database?)

- **Necesitamos mejorar nuestra seguridad informática.** (We need to improve our cybersecurity.)
- **Vamos a lanzar una campaña digital en...** (We're going to launch a digital campaign on...)
- **¿Cuál es la estrategia de SEO para nuestro sitio web?** (What is the SEO strategy for our website?)

Practice Exercise

1. **Tech Project Description:** Describe a tech project you're working on or interested in. Include details about the technology used, the objectives, and the potential impact.
2. **Digital Media Plan:** Outline a plan for a digital media campaign for a product or service. Discuss the platforms you'll use, the target audience, and key messaging.

Tips for Navigating IT and Digital Media Language

- **Keep Learning:** The fields of IT and digital media are fast-evolving. Stay updated with the latest terminology by following industry news and participating in relevant forums or discussions.
- **Practice with Projects:** Apply your technical vocabulary by working on real or hypothetical projects. This contextual learning can reinforce your understanding and retention of terms.
- **Network with Professionals:** Engage with Spanish-speaking professionals in IT and digital media. Conversations with peers can introduce you to new terminology and practices.

Cultural Insight

The digital divide remains a significant issue globally, including in Spanish-speaking countries. Discussions about IT and digital media often touch on topics of access, equity, and the role of technology in societal progress. Understanding these contexts can add depth to your conversations and professional interactions in the field.

Congratulations on completing Day 82! You've expanded your technical vocabulary in the crucial areas of IT and digital media, preparing you for more nuanced conversations and professional activities in these fields. As technology continues to shape our world, your ability to discuss these topics in Spanish will be an invaluable asset. Tomorrow, we'll explore environmental science and sustainability language, further broadening your technical Spanish skills. ¡Hasta mañana!

Day 83: Medical Spanish for Healthcare

Welcome to Day 83, where we focus on Medical Spanish, an essential skill for healthcare professionals and anyone interested in medical conversations. Whether you're working in a healthcare setting, studying medicine, or simply want to discuss health-related topics more effectively, understanding medical terminology and phrases in Spanish can greatly enhance communication with Spanish-speaking patients or colleagues. Today, we'll cover key medical vocabulary, common conditions, and phrases useful in healthcare contexts.

Key Medical Vocabulary

- **La salud** (Health)

- **El médico/la médica** (Doctor)

- **El enfermero/la enfermera** (Nurse)

- **El hospital** (Hospital)

- **La clínica** (Clinic)

- **La farmacia** (Pharmacy)

- **La enfermedad** (Disease)

- **El síntoma** (Symptom)

- **El tratamiento** (Treatment)

- **La medicina** (Medicine)

- **La cirugía** (Surgery)
- **La emergencia** (Emergency)
- **La cita médica** (Medical appointment)

Common Conditions and Symptoms

- **La gripe** (The flu)
- **El resfriado** (The cold)
- **La fiebre** (Fever)
- **El dolor de cabeza** (Headache)
- **La alergia** (Allergy)
- **La hipertensión** (Hypertension)
- **La diabetes** (Diabetes)

Phrases for Healthcare Conversations

- **¿Qué síntomas tiene?** (What symptoms do you have?)
- **¿Desde cuándo se siente así?** (Since when have you been feeling this way?)
- **Necesitamos hacerle unos análisis.** (We need to do some tests on you.)
- **¿Tiene alguna alergia?** (Do you have any allergies?)
- **¿Está tomando alguna medicación?** (Are you taking any medication?)

Practice Exercise

1. **Patient-Doctor Dialogue:** Write a dialogue between a patient and a doctor discussing a health concern. Include questions a doctor might ask and how a patient might describe their symptoms and medical history.

2. **Medical Scenario Role-play:** With a partner, practice a role-play based on a common medical scenario, such as a patient seeking advice at a pharmacy or making a doctor's appointment. Switch roles to experience both perspectives.

Tips for Medical Spanish

- **Clarity and Simplicity:** Use clear, simple language when discussing medical topics, especially with patients. Avoid jargon that may confuse non-medical individuals.

- **Cultural Competence:** Be aware of cultural beliefs and practices related to health and medicine in different Spanish-speaking communities.

- **Continuous Learning:** Medical terminology is vast and constantly evolving. Engage in ongoing learning through medical Spanish courses, textbooks, and professional interactions.

Cultural Insight

In Spanish-speaking cultures, personal rapport and trust are particularly important in healthcare settings. Patients often expect a more personal connection with their healthcare providers, and showing empathy and respect can significantly impact patient comfort and cooperation.

Congratulations on completing Day 83! You've taken a significant step towards bridging communication gaps in healthcare through Medical Spanish. Whether in clinical settings, public health discussions, or personal conversations, these skills are invaluable for providing support and understanding to Spanish-speaking patients. Tomorrow, we'll delve into legal Spanish, enhancing your ability to navigate the legal system or discuss legal matters in Spanish. ¡Hasta mañana!

Day 84: Spanish for Educators and Students

Welcome to Day 84, dedicated to Spanish for educators and students. In the realms of education and learning, being able to communicate effectively in Spanish can greatly enhance the educational experience, whether you're teaching Spanish, teaching in a Spanish-speaking environment, or studying as part of an academic program. Today, we'll explore essential vocabulary, phrases, and concepts relevant to educators and students navigating the educational landscape in Spanish-speaking contexts.

Key Vocabulary for Educators and Students

- **El maestro/la maestra** (Teacher)
- **El estudiante/la estudiante** (Student)
- **La escuela** (School)
- **El colegio** (High school/college)
- **La universidad** (University)
- **La clase** (Class)
- **El curso** (Course)
- **La asignatura/la materia** (Subject)
- **El examen** (Exam)
- **La tarea** (Homework)

- **El horario** (Schedule)
- **La beca** (Scholarship)
- **El semestre** (Semester)
- **El aula** (Classroom)

Phrases for the Educational Setting

- **¿En qué puedo ayudarte?** (How can I help you?)
- **Necesito más práctica en...** (I need more practice in...)
- **¿Puedes explicar eso otra vez?** (Can you explain that again?)
- **Tengo una pregunta sobre...** (I have a question about...)
- **La tarea para mañana es...** (The homework for tomorrow is...)

Expressing Academic Interests and Goals

- **Me interesa estudiar...** (I'm interested in studying...)
- **Mi objetivo es especializarme en...** (My goal is to specialize in...)
- **Quiero mejorar mi nivel de español.** (I want to improve my level of Spanish.)

Practice Exercise

1. **Educational Dialogue:** Create a dialogue between a teacher and a student discussing progress in a specific subject. Include questions about understanding material, suggestions for improvement, and encouragement.

2. **Academic Goals Presentation:** Prepare a short presentation in Spanish outlining your academic interests, goals, and plans for achieving them. This can be shared in a classroom setting or with a language exchange partner.

Tips for Educators and Students

- **Interactive Learning:** Incorporate interactive methods into teaching and learning, such as group discussions, projects, and presentations, to encourage active use of Spanish.

- **Cultural Integration:** Include cultural aspects of Spanish-speaking countries in the curriculum or study plan to enrich the learning experience and foster cultural appreciation.

- **Feedback and Reflection:** Regular feedback and reflective practices can help identify areas of strength and improvement, facilitating targeted learning strategies.

Cultural Insight

Education styles and expectations can vary significantly across Spanish-speaking cultures. Understanding and respecting these differences is crucial for educators and students alike. In many Spanish-speaking countries, there's a strong emphasis on respect for authority in the classroom, collaborative learning, and the importance of education as a pathway to success.

Congratulations on completing Day 84! You've gained valuable insights and tools for navigating educational contexts in Spanish, enhancing both teaching and learning experiences. Whether you're an educator designing engaging lessons or a student pursuing academic excellence, these skills will serve you well in reaching your educational objectives. Tomorrow, we'll explore Spanish for engineering and technology, expanding your professional vocabulary further. ¡Hasta mañana!

Day 85: Legal Spanish and Understanding Contracts

Welcome to Day 85, focused on Legal Spanish and understanding contracts. Navigating legal documents, discussions, and contexts requires a specific set of vocabulary and an understanding of formal language structures. This knowledge is crucial for professionals involved in legal fields, business negotiations, or anyone needing to understand legal agreements in Spanish. Today, we'll introduce key legal terminology and phrases to help you comprehend and discuss contracts and legal matters more effectively.

Key Legal Vocabulary

- **El derecho** (Law)

- **El abogado/la abogada** (Lawyer)

- **El contrato** (Contract)

- **La cláusula** (Clause)

- **El acuerdo** (Agreement)

- **La ley** (Law)

- **El juicio** (Trial)

- **La demanda** (Lawsuit)

- **El demandante** (Plaintiff)

- **El demandado** (Defendant)

- **La firma** (Signature)

- **La validez** (Validity)

- **El testigo** (Witness)

- **El documento legal** (Legal document)

Phrases for Discussing Contracts

- **¿Podría revisar este contrato?** (Could you review this contract?)

- **Esta cláusula especifica que...** (This clause specifies that...)

- **¿Cuál es el plazo del acuerdo?** (What is the term of the agreement?)

- **¿Podemos modificar esta parte del contrato?** (Can we modify this part of the contract?)

- **Necesitamos la firma de todas las partes involucradas.** (We need the signature of all parties involved.)

Understanding Contractual Terms

When reviewing or discussing contracts, it's important to pay attention to:

- **Obligaciones y derechos** (Obligations and rights) - What each party is required to do and is entitled to.

- **Condiciones y términos** (Conditions and terms) - Specific requirements and definitions of key terms.

- **Consecuencias de incumplimiento** (Consequences of non-compliance) - Penalties or actions resulting from not fulfilling the contract.

Practice Exercise

1. **Contract Analysis:** Choose a simple contract or agreement template in Spanish, such as a rental agreement or service contract. Identify and summarize the key clauses, focusing on obligations, rights, and terms.

2. **Legal Scenario Role-play:** Create a role-play scenario where you discuss the terms of a contract with a lawyer or a contracting party. Practice negotiating terms and asking clarifying questions about legal implications.

Tips for Navigating Legal Spanish

- **Precision is Key:** Legal language requires precision. Ensure you understand the exact meaning of terms and phrases.

- **Seek Professional Advice:** When in doubt, consult with a legal professional to avoid misunderstandings.

- **Practice with Real Documents:** Analyze real legal documents to familiarize yourself with common structures and language used.

Cultural Insight

Legal systems vary significantly across Spanish-speaking countries, influenced by history, culture, and governance. Understanding the legal context of the specific country you're dealing with can provide valuable insights and help navigate legal discussions more effectively.

Congratulations on completing Day 85! You've taken a crucial step towards understanding Legal Spanish, enhancing your ability to engage with contracts and legal discussions confidently. Whether for personal or professional reasons, this knowledge empowers you to navigate legal landscapes more effectively. Tomorrow, we'll focus on Spanish for public services and government interactions, further broadening your communicative abilities in specialized contexts. ¡Hasta mañana!

Days 86-90: Professional Language Skills Review

As we approach the final stretch of Part 9, it's time to consolidate and reflect on the professional language skills we've developed. These last days are dedicated to reviewing and applying the specialized vocabulary and conversational strategies relevant to various professional and technical fields. Through comprehensive exercises and practical applications, we'll ensure you're prepared to use your Spanish skills confidently in your career and beyond.

Day 86: Business and Commerce Language Consolidation

- **Exercise:** Draft a business proposal or executive summary for a new venture or project, incorporating the business and commerce vocabulary you've learned. Focus on clarity, persuasiveness, and the correct use of technical terms.

- **Discussion:** Present your proposal in a mock business meeting with peers or a language tutor. Engage in a Q&A session to defend your ideas and demonstrate your command of business Spanish.

Day 87: IT and Digital Media Vocabulary Application

- **Exercise:** Create a blog post, article, or presentation on a current trend in technology or digital media, using the specialized vocabulary from Day 82. Aim to inform, engage, and spark discussion among Spanish-speaking readers or viewers.

- **Interactive Task:** Participate in an online forum or social media group focused on IT or digital media topics in Spanish. Share your insights, ask questions, and interact with other members to practice your technical language skills.

Day 88: Medical Spanish in Practice

- **Exercise:** Simulate a patient consultation or medical conference presentation, employing the medical vocabulary and phrases you've studied. Describe symptoms, diagnoses, treatments, or recent medical advancements.

- **Role-play:** With a partner, practice a medical role-play scenario, alternating roles between healthcare provider and patient. Focus on accurate use of medical terms, empathetic communication, and clarity in explanations.

Day 89: Legal Spanish and Contract Negotiations

- **Exercise:** Analyze a legal document or contract in Spanish, identifying key clauses, rights, and obligations. Summarize your findings and suggest any amendments for clarity or improved fairness.

- **Negotiation Simulation:** Engage in a simulated negotiation over a contract's terms with a peer or tutor. Practice articulating your points, making concessions, and ultimately reaching an agreement using precise legal Spanish.

Day 90: Culmination Project: Multidisciplinary Spanish Presentation

- **Project:** Prepare a comprehensive presentation that integrates topics from business, technology, medicine, and law, demonstrating your proficiency in professional and technical Spanish. Choose a theme that allows you to explore the interconnectivity of these fields, such as launching a tech startup, discussing a public health initiative, or exploring the impact of digital innovation on business and legal practices.

- **Presentation:** Deliver your presentation to an audience, real or simulated, and engage in a discussion about your topic. Focus on delivering clear, concise information, responding to questions, and showcasing your specialized vocabulary and conversational skills.

Final Reflection

Reflect on your progress and the practical applications of the Spanish language in your professional life. Consider areas for further development and set goals for continuing to enhance your language skills.

Congratulations on completing the Professional Language Skills Review of Part 9! You've demonstrated a remarkable commitment to mastering Spanish in professional and technical contexts. Continue to practice, stay curious, and seek opportunities to use Spanish in your career and daily life. Your efforts will open doors to new opportunities and deepen your connections in the Spanish-speaking world. ¡Felicidades y adelante con tu éxito profesional!

Part 10: Days 91-100 - Mastery and Beyond

Day 91: Creative Writing and Storytelling

Welcome to Day 91, where we delve into creative writing and storytelling in Spanish. This stage is all about using the language to express imagination, convey emotions, and engage audiences through compelling narratives. Creative writing in Spanish not only enhances your linguistic skills but also provides a deeper understanding of cultural nuances and storytelling traditions. Today, we'll explore techniques and prompts to inspire your storytelling and creative writing journey.

Techniques for Creative Writing in Spanish

- **Show, Don't Tell:** Use descriptive language to create vivid images in the reader's mind. Instead of simply stating facts, illustrate them through sensory details and actions.

- **Dialogue:** Incorporate realistic dialogue to give voice to your characters and advance the plot. Remember to use authentic expressions and regional slang where appropriate.

- **Conflict and Resolution:** Build your story around a central conflict or challenge and guide your characters towards a resolution. This creates tension and keeps readers engaged.

- **Cultural Elements:** Weave cultural references, settings, and themes into your narratives to enrich your stories and provide authentic Spanish-speaking context.

Story Prompts to Get Started

1. **A Magical Encounter:** Write a story about someone who discovers an ancient object in a local market, which leads to unexpected magical events.

2. **Cross-Cultural Journey:** Narrate the adventures of a character traveling through various Spanish-speaking countries, highlighting the unique cultural experiences in each.

3. **Historical Fiction:** Create a tale set in a significant historical period of a Spanish-speaking country, blending historical facts with fictional elements.

4. **Future Visions:** Imagine a future scenario influenced by current social or environmental issues in the Spanish-speaking world and describe how characters navigate this future.

Practice Exercise

- Choose one of the story prompts above or come up with your own. Outline your story, focusing on the setting, characters, and plot. Write a short story or the first chapter of a longer piece, incorporating the creative writing techniques discussed.

- Share your story with peers, a writing group, or a tutor. Ask for feedback on language use, creativity, and cultural accuracy.

Tips for Creative Writing and Storytelling

- **Read Widely:** Immerse yourself in a variety of Spanish literature and media to gain inspiration and understand different writing styles.

- **Experiment:** Don't be afraid to try out different genres, perspectives, and narrative voices to discover what works best for you.

- **Revise:** Revising is a crucial part of the writing process. Review your work for coherence, grammar, and style improvements.

Cultural Insight

Storytelling is a powerful medium in Spanish-speaking cultures, often used to preserve history, share wisdom, and celebrate cultural identity. Engaging with storytelling traditions can deepen your appreciation of the language and enrich your creative expressions.

Congratulations on completing Day 91! By exploring creative writing and storytelling, you're unlocking new dimensions of language mastery, allowing for personal expression and cultural exploration. Continue to nurture your creativity and practice your storytelling skills, and you'll find that Spanish offers a rich tapestry of narratives waiting to be told. Tomorrow, we'll delve into advanced language techniques, further enhancing your ability to express complex ideas and emotions in Spanish.

Day 92: Debates, Opinions, and Critical Thinking

Welcome to Day 92, dedicated to sharpening your skills in debates, expressing opinions, and employing critical thinking in Spanish. Engaging in debates and discussing various viewpoints are excellent ways to deepen your understanding of issues, articulate your thoughts clearly, and interact meaningfully in Spanish. Today, we'll explore strategies for effective argumentation, presenting opinions, and fostering critical discussions.

Strategies for Effective Debates and Argumentation

- **Construct a Clear Argument:** Begin with a clear statement of your position. Use logical reasoning to support your viewpoint, drawing on relevant facts, examples, and evidence.

- **Acknowledge Opposing Views:** Demonstrating awareness of alternative perspectives enhances the credibility of your argument. Consider counterarguments and address them respectfully.

- **Use Persuasive Language:** Employ persuasive expressions and rhetorical techniques to strengthen your case. Phrases like *en mi opinión* (in my opinion), *lo que indica que* (which indicates that), and *a pesar de* (despite) can be useful.

- **Stay Informed:** A well-informed argument is more compelling. Stay updated on current events, research, and cultural insights related to the topics you discuss.

Expressing Opinions and Critical Thinking

- **Expressing Opinions:** Start your sentences with phrases like *Creo que...* (I believe that...), *Pienso que...* (I think that...), or *Opino que...* (I opine that...) to clearly state your opinions.

- **Encouraging Discussion:** Ask open-ended questions to encourage dialogue and explore different viewpoints. Use questions like *¿Qué opinas tú?* (What do you think?) or *¿Cómo ves...?* (How do you see...?).

- **Critical Analysis:** When analyzing statements, issues, or beliefs, use critical thinking to question assumptions, evaluate evidence, and consider implications. Phrases like *Es crucial examinar...* (It's crucial to examine...) or *Es necesario cuestionar...* (It's necessary to question...) can be helpful.

Practice Exercise

1. **Debate Preparation:** Choose a contemporary issue relevant to the Spanish-speaking world. Research the topic to understand different perspectives and prepare your argument, including supporting evidence and potential counterarguments.

2. **Discussion and Debate:** Organize a debate or discussion group session. Present your arguments, listen to and respectfully challenge others, and engage in a collaborative exploration of the topic.

Tips for Engaging in Discussions

- **Listen Actively:** Understanding others' viewpoints is as important as articulating your own. Listen carefully to respond thoughtfully and constructively.

- **Embrace Complexity:** Many issues don't have clear-cut answers. Acknowledge the complexity and nuance in discussions.

- **Practice Tolerance:** Respect for diverse opinions fosters a healthy environment for debate and discussion. Aim for understanding, even when you disagree.

Cultural Insight

Debates and discussions in Spanish-speaking cultures can be lively and passionate, reflecting a strong tradition of oral expression and public discourse. Understanding cultural contexts and sensitivities is key to engaging effectively and respectfully.

Congratulations on completing Day 92! You've enhanced your ability to participate in debates, express opinions, and engage in critical thinking in Spanish. These skills not only elevate your linguistic proficiency but also enrich your cultural understanding and interpersonal interactions. Tomorrow, we'll explore nuances in language that convey emotion, tone, and subtlety, further refining your mastery of Spanish.

Day 93: Public Speaking and Presentations

Welcome to Day 93, focusing on public speaking and presentations in Spanish. Whether it's delivering a speech, presenting a project, or leading a meeting, effective public speaking skills are essential for clearly communicating your ideas and engaging your audience. Today, we'll cover techniques for successful presentations and the specific language tools that can enhance your public speaking endeavors in Spanish.

Techniques for Successful Presentations

- **Know Your Audience:** Tailor your language, examples, and content to the interests and level of understanding of your audience.

- **Clear Structure:** Organize your presentation with a clear introduction, body, and conclusion. Use transitions to connect ideas smoothly.

- **Engaging Content:** Incorporate stories, anecdotes, or relevant questions to engage the audience and make your points more relatable.

- **Visual Aids:** Use slides, images, or videos judiciously to complement your spoken words, not replace them.

Vocabulary for Public Speaking

- **La presentación** (Presentation)
- **El discurso** (Speech)

- **El público** (Audience)
- **La conferencia** (Lecture, conference)
- **El ponente/la ponente** (Speaker)
- **El tema** (Topic)
- **Los puntos clave** (Key points)
- **La diapositiva** (Slide)
- **La conclusión** (Conclusion)
- **La pregunta** (Question)
- **La respuesta** (Answer)

Phrases to Structure Your Presentation

- **Para empezar/comenzar...** (To start/begin...)
- **En cuanto a...** (Regarding...)
- **Lo más importante es...** (The most important thing is...)
- **Además...** (Furthermore...)
- **Por último/Para concluir...** (Lastly/To conclude...)

Engaging the Audience

- **¿Qué opinan ustedes de...?** (What do you all think of...?)
- **Quisiera destacar que...** (I would like to highlight that...)
- **Como pueden ver...** (As you can see...)
- **Les invito a reflexionar sobre...** (I invite you to reflect on...)

Practice Exercise

1. **Prepare a Presentation:** Choose a topic you're passionate about related to Spanish-speaking cultures, societies, or any area of professional interest. Outline your presentation, including key vocabulary, phrases to structure your speech, and ideas for engaging the audience.

2. **Deliver and Record:** Deliver your presentation to a group, real or simulated, and record it if possible. Pay attention to your use of Spanish, body language, and audience engagement techniques.

Tips for Effective Public Speaking

- **Practice:** Rehearse your presentation multiple times to gain fluency and confidence.

- **Pace Yourself:** Speak clearly and at a pace that allows your audience to absorb the information.

- **Feedback:** Seek feedback from listeners to identify strengths and areas for improvement.

Cultural Insight

Public speaking in Spanish-speaking cultures values clarity, emotion, and a connection with the audience. Personal stories or references to shared cultural experiences can greatly enhance the receptiveness of your audience.

Congratulations on completing Day 93! Mastering public speaking and presentation skills in Spanish significantly boosts your ability to communicate effectively in professional and social settings. Continue practicing these skills, seeking opportunities to present and share your ideas in Spanish. Tomorrow, we'll explore advanced negotiation techniques, further enhancing your proficiency in professional Spanish interactions.

Day 94: Understanding and Analyzing Media

Welcome to Day 94, where we focus on understanding and analyzing media in Spanish. In today's globalized world, being able to critically engage with media—news articles, broadcasts, social media content, and more—is crucial for informed citizenship and cultural literacy. This lesson will equip you with the tools to dissect media messages, understand different perspectives, and discuss media content effectively in Spanish.

Key Vocabulary for Media Analysis

- **Los medios de comunicación** (Media)

- **La noticia** (News)

- **El artículo** (Article)

- **El reportaje** (Report)

- **El periodista** (Journalist)

- **La fuente** (Source)

- **El titular** (Headline)

- **El punto de vista** (Point of view)

- **La opinión** (Opinion)

- **El hecho** (Fact)

- **La perspectiva** (Perspective)

- **La parcialidad** (Bias)
- **La audiencia** (Audience)
- **El análisis** (Analysis)

Strategies for Media Analysis

- **Identify the Main Idea:** What is the primary message or information the piece is trying to convey?
- **Distinguish Between Facts and Opinions:** Separate objective information from the author's or publication's perspective.
- **Consider the Source:** Who produced the content, and what might be their motivation?
- **Analyze the Language:** How does the choice of words, tone, and style influence the message?
- **Recognize Bias:** Is there an apparent bias, and how does it affect the portrayal of events or issues?

Phrases for Discussing Media Content

- **Según este artículo...** (According to this article...)
- **El autor argumenta que...** (The author argues that...)
- **Una perspectiva interesante es...** (An interesting perspective is...)
- **Esto plantea la cuestión de...** (This raises the question of...)
- **Es evidente que hay un sesgo...** (It's evident that there is a bias...)

Practice Exercise

1. **Media Analysis Activity:** Choose a current news article or report in Spanish from a reputable source. Read it carefully and write an analysis covering the points mentioned above. Share your analysis in a discussion group or class setting, inviting comments and perspectives.

2. **Debate on Media Issues:** Organize a debate on a media-related issue highlighted in the article, such as media bias, the role of journalism in society, or the impact of social media on public opinion. Use the vocabulary and phrases learned to articulate your points clearly.

Tips for Engaging with Media in Spanish

- **Diverse Sources:** Consume media from a variety of Spanish-speaking countries and outlets to get a broad perspective on issues.

- **Active Engagement:** Don't just passively consume media. Take notes, ask questions, and seek to engage with the content critically.

- **Language Learning:** Use media as a tool to improve your Spanish skills, noting new vocabulary, expressions, and grammatical structures.

Cultural Insight

Media in Spanish-speaking countries plays a pivotal role in shaping public opinion, culture, and political landscapes. Understanding regional dialects, slang, and cultural references can enhance your comprehension and appreciation of the subtleties in media content.

Congratulations on completing Day 94! By learning to critically analyze media in Spanish, you've gained not only a deeper understanding of the language but also insights into the cultures and societies of Spanish-speaking countries. This skill is invaluable for navigating the modern world's complex information landscape. Tomorrow, we will delve into the use of Spanish in science and research, expanding your technical vocabulary and application of Spanish in academic contexts.

Day 95: The Path to Bilingualism – Next Steps

Welcome to Day 95, where we focus on the journey towards bilingualism and the next steps you can take to solidify your mastery of Spanish while embracing a bilingual lifestyle. Achieving fluency is a significant milestone, but true bilingualism involves continuous learning, cultural immersion, and applying your skills in varied contexts. Today, we'll explore strategies to deepen your connection with the Spanish language and ensure your skills not only remain sharp but also evolve.

Strategies for Deepening Bilingualism

- **Immersive Experiences:** Seek opportunities for immersion, such as traveling to Spanish-speaking countries, attending cultural events, or participating in language exchange programs.

- **Professional Use:** Incorporate Spanish into your professional life by pursuing job opportunities that require bilingualism, offering to translate or interpret, or engaging with Spanish-speaking clients and colleagues.

- **Educational Advancement:** Consider furthering your education in Spanish by taking advanced courses, attending workshops, or even pursuing a degree in Spanish language studies or a related field.

- **Creative Expression:** Use Spanish as a medium for creative expression through writing, art, music, or content creation. Sharing your work can connect you with a community and provide feedback.

Next Steps in Your Language Journey

- **Set New Goals:** Identify new areas of interest in the language, whether it's mastering a specific dialect, learning about a particular cultural aspect, or acquiring technical vocabulary in a field of expertise.

- **Mentorship and Teaching:** Share your knowledge by tutoring beginners, volunteering in language teaching programs, or creating educational content. Teaching is a powerful way to solidify your own skills.

- **Continuous Learning:** Languages evolve, and staying informed about changes and new expressions keeps your skills current. Subscribe to Spanish-language publications, podcasts, and channels.

- **Cultural Participation:** Deepen your cultural understanding by engaging with the Spanish-speaking community. Attend cultural festivals, read Spanish literature, watch Spanish films, and participate in discussions.

Practice Exercise

- **Language and Culture Project:** Develop a project that combines language skills with cultural exploration. This could be a research paper on a sociolinguistic topic, a series of blog posts about regional cuisines, or a video documentary on a cultural phenomenon.

- **Presentation and Discussion:** Present your project to a group or community interested in Spanish language learning. Use this as an opportunity to discuss, receive feedback, and engage in deep conversations about the language and culture.

Maintaining and Advancing Fluency

- **Daily Practice:** Incorporate Spanish into your daily routine, from switching your phone's language to Spanish to listening to Spanish music or podcasts during your commute.

- **Networking:** Join professional or social networks that connect Spanish speakers and language learners. Engaging in regular conversation is key to maintaining fluency.

Cultural Insight

Bilingualism opens a window to the world, offering insights into the lives, thoughts, and hearts of people across cultures. Embrace the responsibility to use your language skills to foster understanding, empathy, and connection between communities.

Congratulations on completing Day 95! Your commitment to achieving and advancing bilingualism is a testament to your dedication to personal and professional growth. Remember, the journey of language learning is infinite, with each step offering new opportunities for discovery and connection. Continue to explore, engage, and enjoy the rich tapestry of experiences that bilingualism brings. Tomorrow, we'll explore strategies for lifelong language learning and staying connected to the Spanish-speaking world.

Days 96-100: Final Review and Path Forward

As we approach the conclusion of our journey through Part 10, these last days are dedicated to reviewing what we've learned, celebrating our achievements, and planning our path forward. The mastery of Spanish you've developed is not just a testament to your hard work but also a foundation for continued growth, exploration, and connection. Let's reflect on key takeaways, reinforce our learning, and envision the next steps in our lifelong language journey.

Day 96: Reflecting on Achievements

- **Reflective Writing:** Write a reflective essay on your language learning journey. Include challenges you've overcome, milestones you've reached, and how your relationship with the Spanish language and culture has evolved.

- **Sharing Session:** Share your reflections with your language learning community, peers, or mentor. Discuss your experiences, insights, and the impact of bilingualism on your personal and professional life.

Day 97: Strengthening Weak Areas

- **Identify and Address:** Review your notes and feedback received throughout this journey to identify areas needing further improvement, such as specific grammar topics, vocabulary, or conversational skills.

- **Focused Practice:** Dedicate today to intensive practice in these areas. Utilize exercises, language apps, or conversations with native speakers to reinforce your understanding and skills.

Day 98: Cultural Immersion and Continued Learning

- **Cultural Exploration:** Choose a Spanish-speaking culture you're particularly interested in but haven't explored in-depth. Dedicate the day to learning about its history, art, music, cuisine, and social norms.

- **Language Meetup:** Organize or attend a language exchange meetup focused on the culture you explored. Share your learnings, ask questions, and practice discussing cultural topics in Spanish.

Day 99: Setting Future Goals

- **Goal-Setting Session:** Reflect on your future aspirations related to Spanish. Consider goals like achieving fluency in another dialect, mastering a professional domain in Spanish, or engaging in translation work.

- **Action Plan:** Create a detailed plan for achieving these goals. Include resources needed, milestones, and a timeline. Consider how you'll integrate Spanish practice into your daily life for continuous improvement.

Day 100: Celebrating Your Journey

- **Celebration of Learning:** Organize a celebration of your language learning journey. This could be a Spanish-themed dinner, a presentation of your projects, or a storytelling session recounting your experiences and learnings.

- **Commitment to Lifelong Learning:** Write a commitment letter to yourself, outlining your dedication to ongoing learning and engagement with the Spanish language and its many cultures. Seal it and set a future date to reopen and reflect on your progress.

Path Forward

- **Lifelong Learning:** Commit to making Spanish a living part of your life through regular practice, cultural engagement, and professional use.

- **Community Engagement:** Continue to be an active member of language and cultural communities, offering support to fellow learners and seeking out mentorship opportunities.

- **Advocacy and Teaching:** Use your skills to advocate for and teach others about the importance of language learning and cross-cultural communication.

Congratulations on completing the final review and envisioning your path forward! You've not only achieved a remarkable level of Spanish proficiency but also laid the groundwork for continuous growth and exploration. Remember, mastery is not a destination but a journey—one that enriches your life with every step. Celebrate your accomplishments, embrace new challenges with enthusiasm, and carry forward the joy of learning into all your future endeavors. ¡Felicidades y adelante siempre!

Appendix A: Commonly Confused Words

The journey of learning Spanish involves navigating through a sea of words that may look or sound similar but carry different meanings. Understanding these commonly confused words is crucial for clear communication and to avoid misunderstandings. Here's a guide to some of the frequently mixed-up terms in Spanish, providing clarity and helping to refine your usage.

1. Aceptar (to accept) vs. Exceptuar (to except)

- **Aceptar** means to agree to or receive something willingly.
  - *He aceptado el trabajo.* (I have accepted the job.)
- **Exceptuar** means to exclude something from a general rule.
  - *Todos fueron invitados, exceptuando a Luis.* (Everyone was invited, except Luis.)

2. Aconsejar (to advise) vs. Avisar (to inform)

- **Aconsejar** means to give advice or counsel.
  - *Mi profesor me aconsejó estudiar más.* (My teacher advised me to study more.)
- **Avisar** means to notify or inform about something.
  - *Te avisaré cuando estén listos los documentos.* (I will inform you when the documents are ready.)

3. Asistir (to attend) vs. Atender (to assist/to attend to)

- **Asistir** means to be present at an event or meeting.
  - *Asistí a la conferencia ayer.* (I attended the conference yesterday.)
- **Atender** means to take care of or provide service to someone.
  - *El médico atendió al paciente de inmediato.* (The doctor attended to the patient immediately.)

4. Bizarro (brave) vs. Bizarre (strange)

- **Bizarro** in Spanish means brave or gallant, a false friend with the English "bizarre."
  - *El caballero era conocido por su actitud bizarra.* (The knight was known for his brave attitude.)
- The correct term for the English "bizarre" is **extraño** or **raro**.
  - *Fue una situación bastante extraña.* (It was a quite bizarre situation.)

5. Comida (meal/food) vs. Comedia (comedy)

- **Comida** refers to a meal or food in general.
  - *La comida española es mi favorita.* (Spanish food is my favorite.)
- **Comedia** means a comedic play, movie, or show.
  - *Nos reímos mucho con esa comedia.* (We laughed a lot at that comedy.)

6. Descripción (description) vs. Prescripción (prescription)

- **Descripción** refers to the act of describing something.

- *La descripción del lugar era precisa.* (The description of the place was accurate.)
- **Prescripción** refers to a medical prescription or the act of prescribing.
  - *Necesito ir a la farmacia a recoger una prescripción.* (I need to go to the pharmacy to pick up a prescription.)

7. Embarazada (pregnant) vs. Avergonzada (embarrassed)

- **Embarazada** means pregnant, a common false friend with the English "embarrassed."
  - *Ella está embarazada de tres meses.* (She is three months pregnant.)
- **Avergonzada** is the correct term for feeling ashamed or embarrassed.
  - *Estaba avergonzada por haber llegado tarde.* (She was embarrassed for being late.)

8. Actualmente (currently) vs. Actualidad (present time)

- **Actualmente** refers to something happening at the current time.
  - *Actualmente, vivo en Madrid.* (I currently live in Madrid.)
- **Actualidad** refers to the concept of the present time or period.
  - *En la actualidad, la tecnología avanza rápidamente.* (In the present time, technology is advancing rapidly.)

This list is by no means exhaustive but offers insight into some of the common pitfalls learners might encounter. Understanding these distinctions is key to enhancing your fluency and confidence in Spanish. Keep exploring and practicing, and over time, navigating these nuances will become second nature.

APPENDIX B: VERB CONJUGATION TABLES

Verb conjugation is foundational to expressing ideas in Spanish, as it allows you to articulate actions across different tenses and subjects. Below are tables for the conjugation of regular verbs ending in -ar, -er, and -ir in the present, past (preterite), and future tenses, providing a clear reference for these essential forms.

Regular -ar Verbs Conjugation (e.g., "hablar" - to speak)

Subject	Present	Preterite	Future
yo	hablo	hablé	hablaré
tú	hablas	hablaste	hablarás
él/ella	habla	habló	hablará
nosotros	hablamos	hablamos	hablaremos
vosotros	habláis	hablasteis	hablaréis
ellos	hablan	hablaron	hablarán

Regular -er Verbs Conjugation (e.g., "comer" - to eat)

Subject	Present	Preterite	Future
yo	como	comí	comeré
tú	comes	comiste	comerás
él/ella	come	comió	comerá
nosotros	comemos	comimos	comeremos
vosotros	coméis	comisteis	comeréis
ellos	comen	comieron	comerán

Regular -ir Verbs Conjugation (e.g., "vivir" - to live)

Subject	Present	Preterite	Future
yo	vivo	viví	viviré
tú	vives	viviste	vivirás
él/ella	vive	vivió	vivirá
nosotros	vivimos	vivimos	viviremos
vosotros	vivís	vivisteis	viviréis
ellos	viven	vivieron	vivirán

Notes on Usage

- **Present Tense:** Used to describe actions that are currently happening or habitual actions.
- **Preterite Tense:** Used to describe actions that were completed at a definite point in the past.
- **Future Tense:** Used to describe actions that will happen in the future.

Understanding these basic conjugations is crucial for building more complex sentences and expressing a wide range of actions and ideas. Remember, irregular verbs and other tenses (such as the imperfect, subjunctive, and conditional) follow different patterns and are essential for advanced proficiency. Practicing these conjugations in context will greatly improve your fluency and understanding of Spanish verb usage.

Appendix C: Mexican Spanish vs. Spain Spanish

The Spanish language, with its global spread, exhibits a rich tapestry of dialectal variation. Among these, Mexican Spanish and Spain Spanish (often referred to as Castilian) are two of the most widely recognized and studied dialects. Understanding the key differences between them can enhance comprehension and communication for Spanish language learners. Here, we explore some primary distinctions that characterize these two variants of Spanish.

Pronunciation

- **Distinción vs. Seseo:** In most parts of Spain, there's a distinction between the pronunciation of "c" (before "e" or "i") and "z" as a "th" sound (distinción), whereas in Mexico, both are pronounced as an "s" (seseo).

- **Yeísmo:** Both dialects generally practice yeísmo, where "ll" and "y" share the same sound, but the actual sound can vary regionally.

Vocabulary

Differences in vocabulary can sometimes make it seem as though Mexican Spanish and Spain Spanish are very different. Here are a few examples:

- **Car vs. Automobile:** In Mexico, "carro" or "coche" is commonly used, while in Spain, "coche" is the standard word.

- **Computer:** In Spain, "ordenador" is used, whereas in Mexico, it's "computadora."
- **Juice:** "Jugo" is used in Mexico, and "zumo" in Spain.

Grammar and Usage

- **Vosotros vs. Ustedes:** In Spain, "vosotros" is used for the informal second-person plural, while in Mexico (and much of Latin America), "ustedes" is used for both formal and informal plural addresses, and "vosotros" is not used.
- **Past Tense:** There are some differences in past tense usage. In Spain, the present perfect is often used to talk about recent past actions (e.g., "He comido" for "I have eaten"), whereas in Mexico, the simple past is more commonly used for actions in the past, regardless of when they occurred (e.g., "Comí" for "I ate").

Formality and Politeness

- **Tuteo and Usted:** The use of "tú" and "usted" can vary significantly in different contexts, with Spain generally being more liberal with "tú" and Mexico tending to use "usted" in more formal situations to denote respect.

Cultural References

- Language in both countries is deeply intertwined with cultural identity, history, and expressions. Mexican Spanish is rich with indigenous language influences, while Spain Spanish carries elements from its own regional languages and history.

Expressions and Idiomatic Phrases

- Each variant has its own set of idiomatic expressions that reflect cultural nuances. For example, Mexican Spanish is known for its colorful and unique idioms, many of which may not be immediately understood by speakers from Spain, and vice versa.

Conclusion

The differences between Mexican Spanish and Spain Spanish highlight the diversity within the Spanish-speaking world. For learners, exposure to both variants enriches understanding and appreciation of the Spanish language's global complexity. As with any language, immersion, practice, and communication with native speakers are key to navigating these differences effectively.

Glossary of Terms

This comprehensive glossary merges the foundational and extended glossaries, offering a broad spectrum of terms relevant to language learning, cultural nuances, Spanish linguistics, and more. It's designed to be a resource for deepening your understanding of both the linguistic and cultural dimensions of the Spanish-speaking world.

A

- **Accent:** Distinctive way of pronunciation characteristic of a particular region or country.

- **Accentuation:** The manner in which stress or emphasis is applied to syllables in words.

- **Acculturation:** The process of adopting the cultural traits or social patterns of another group.

- **Adjective:** A word that describes or modifies a noun.

- **Adverb:** A word that modifies a verb, an adjective, or another adverb, expressing manner, place, time, or degree.

- **Article:** A word used before a noun to indicate the definiteness or indefiniteness of the noun.

B

- **Bilabial:** A sound produced by bringing both lips together.

- **Bilingual Education:** An educational strategy that involves teaching academic content in two languages.

- **Bilingualism:** The ability to fluently speak two languages.
- **Bilabial:** A sound produced by bringing both lips together.

C

- **Clause:** A group of words containing a subject and predicate, functioning as part of a complex or compound sentence.
- **Code-Switching:** The practice of alternating between two or more languages or dialects within a single conversation or utterance.
- **Cognate:** A word that has a similar form and origin in two languages.
- **Conjugation:** The variation of the form of a verb in accordance with mood, tense, person, and number.
- **Connotation:** An idea or feeling that a word invokes in addition to its literal or primary meaning.
- **Culture:** The social behavior, norms, knowledge, beliefs, arts, laws, customs, and habits of the people in a society.

D

- **Demonstrative Adjective:** An adjective that is used to point out which person or thing is being referred to.
- **Dialect:** A particular form of a language specific to a region or social group.
- **Diphthong:** A sound formed by the combination of two vowels in a single syllable, where one vowel sound glides into another.

E

- **Etymology:** The study of the origin of words and the way in which their meanings have changed throughout history.

- **Exonym:** A name for a place, city, or country in a foreign language.

- **Expat:** Short for expatriate; a person who lives outside their native country.

F

- **False Cognate:** Words in two languages that look or sound similar, but differ significantly in meaning.

- **Fluency:** The ability to speak or write a language easily, accurately, and articulately.

- **Folklore:** The traditional beliefs, customs, and stories of a community, passed through generations by word of mouth.

- **Fricative:** A consonant sound where the flow of air is partially obstructed.

G

- **Gerund:** A verb form that ends in -ing in English and is used as a noun; in Spanish, it ends in -ando or -iendo.

- **Grammar:** The system and structure of a language, including syntax, morphology, and punctuation.

H

- **Homophone:** Two or more words having the same pronunciation but different meanings, origins, or spelling.

- **Hypernym:** A word with a broad meaning that more specific words fall under.

I

- **Idiom:** A phrase or expression whose meaning cannot be understood from the ordinary meanings of the words it is made of.
- **Inflection:** A change in the form of a word (usually the ending) to express a grammatical function or attribute.
- **Interjection:** An exclamation, especially as a part of speech.
- **Intonation:** The rise and fall of the voice in speaking.

L

- **Lexicon:** The vocabulary of a person, language, or branch of knowledge.
- **Linguistics:** The scientific study of language and its structure.

M

- **Modal Verb:** A type of verb that is used to indicate modality.
- **Morphology:** The study of the forms of words.

N

- **Nominalization:** The process of converting a word into a noun.
- **Noun:** A word that functions as the name of a specific object or set of objects.

O

- **Orthography:** The conventional spelling system of a language.

P

- **Palatal:** A sound produced by pressing the tongue against the hard palate.
- **Polysemy:** The coexistence of many possible meanings for a word or phrase.

R

- **Register:** The degree of formality with which language is used.
- **Rhotic:** Relating to or denoting a dialect in which "r" sounds are pronounced.

S

- **Semantics:** The branch of linguistics concerned with meaning.
- **Sibilant:** A hissing sound.

T

- **Tautology:** The saying of the same thing twice in different words.
- **Tense:** The form of a verb that indicates the time of the action.

- **Transliteration:** The process of transferring a word from the alphabet of one language to another.

- **Translation:** The process of translating words or text from one language into another.

V

- **Velar:** A sound produced with the back of the tongue against the soft part of the palate.

- **Verb:** A word used to describe an action, state, or occurrence.

- **Vernacular:** The language or dialect spoken by ordinary people.

- **Vocabulary:** The body of words used in a particular language.

This comprehensive glossary serves as a valuable reference for navigating the complexities of language learning, cultural exploration, and Spanish linguistics. Familiarity with these terms enriches your understanding and enhances your ability to communicate effectively in Spanish.

About The Author

Javier Caminos is a celebrated educator and author renowned for his contributions to language learning and education. With over two decades of experience, Javier has dedicated his career to developing innovative language acquisition strategies that cater to learners at all levels.

Born and raised in Madrid, Spain, Javier's passion for languages and cultures ignited early. He pursued his academic interests at the Universidad Complutense de Madrid, where he earned a degree in Linguistics and a Master's in Education, focusing on second language acquisition. His academic journey provided a solid foundation in both the theoretical aspects of language learning and practical challenges faced by learners.

Javier's teaching philosophy emphasizes practical application, cultural sensitivity, and immersive learning experiences. He has worked closely with universities and language schools, designing curriculum materials, conducting workshops, and leading seminars on language acquisition and cultural competency.

Beyond his educational endeavors, Javier is a prolific writer and speaker. He regularly contributes articles to language learning publications and speaks at conferences worldwide, advocating for the importance of language proficiency in enhancing professional development and fostering understanding across diverse communities.

In his personal time, Javier enjoys traveling, experiencing new cultures, and volunteering in community initiatives. Fluent in Spanish, English, and French, he is currently learning Portuguese, driven by his belief in lifelong learning and the power of languages to connect people across cultures.

Javier Caminos continues to inspire students, educators, and professionals through his dedication to excellence in language education. His work promotes understanding and respect across diverse communities, enriching lives through the transformative power of language.

Made in the USA
Columbia, SC
27 June 2025

8b0863e7-9fc1-4edd-b6ca-2f138c1b3b88R02